Praise for *Songs My Mother Taught Me*

"When you first encounter Saul Williams's passionate prose, it is tempting to call him the voice of his generation. But you would be wrong. Saul Williams is not the voice of his or any other generation. His vision is uniquely his own, deeply rooted in his specific African American identity, but so expansive that it allows him to embrace the world from Brazil to Gaza without missing a beat. His writing is unflinching without being accusatory and, when he articulates the bedrock belief that 'a deep-seated love of humanity lies in the heart of every revolutionary,' you know you can believe him." **—Pearl Cleage**

"Saul Williams is the greatest living poet—a transcendent voice that has dissolved the boundaries between spoken word, revolutionary action, and the interplanetary limits of time and space.

I first saw Saul perform as a teenager in a claustrophobic club in Chicago. I remember feeling assaulted by words, like a Bad Brains performance at CBGB's, though I don't recall there being any music. The controlled, poignantly directed violence of his language burned itself into my artistic memory. Shortly after, I sampled 'Sha-Clack-Clack' on the intro to my very first mixtape.

With an eternal body of work spanning film, literature, music, fashion, and, most importantly, the revolution of culture, Saul represents, for so many of us, the boundless potential of a radical imagination unencumbered by the confines of medium." **—Vic M**

"An urgent offering. Saul Williams reminds us there are no sidelines in our collective struggle for liberation. With extraordinary courage, Williams weaves both memoir and call to arms. *Songs My Mother Taught Me* is a reminder to re-member beyond the histories dismembered by colonization. This book recharges your political battery! He wasn't born like this; this collage of care shines light on the contextual magic necessary to cultivate an artist with an articulated politic rooted in the Black radical tradition.

This book is for anyone in search of a new now, anyone who knows art is a form of weaponry, anyone looking to sharpen their practice into a tool that sculpts new worlds, anyone pulling the thread of tomorrow searching for radical fewtures." **—Def Sound**

"Who must we be in a world premised on individualism and evisceration? In *Songs My Mother Taught Me*, griot Saul Williams reveals the complex ways of knowing and being together that scaffold his radical artistry and global vision. Animated by critical inheritances from Paul Robeson, Amiri Baraka, and others, he writes our frightening and vulnerable present with courage and clarity, and the urgent reminder that things need not be this way. Rebellion is a choice within reach. Beyond announcing who Saul is, this book asks who the fuck you are." **—Shana L. Redmond**

"Powerful, generous, and brilliantly tender, rejecting the generational amnesia the empire requires to survive. Saul examines art as an inherently political force, exploring what responsibility the artist bears in moments of crisis—compliance or resistance? Exquisite and essential reading for the revolution from one of our greatest minds."

—Warsan Shire

SONGS MY MOTHER TAUGHT ME

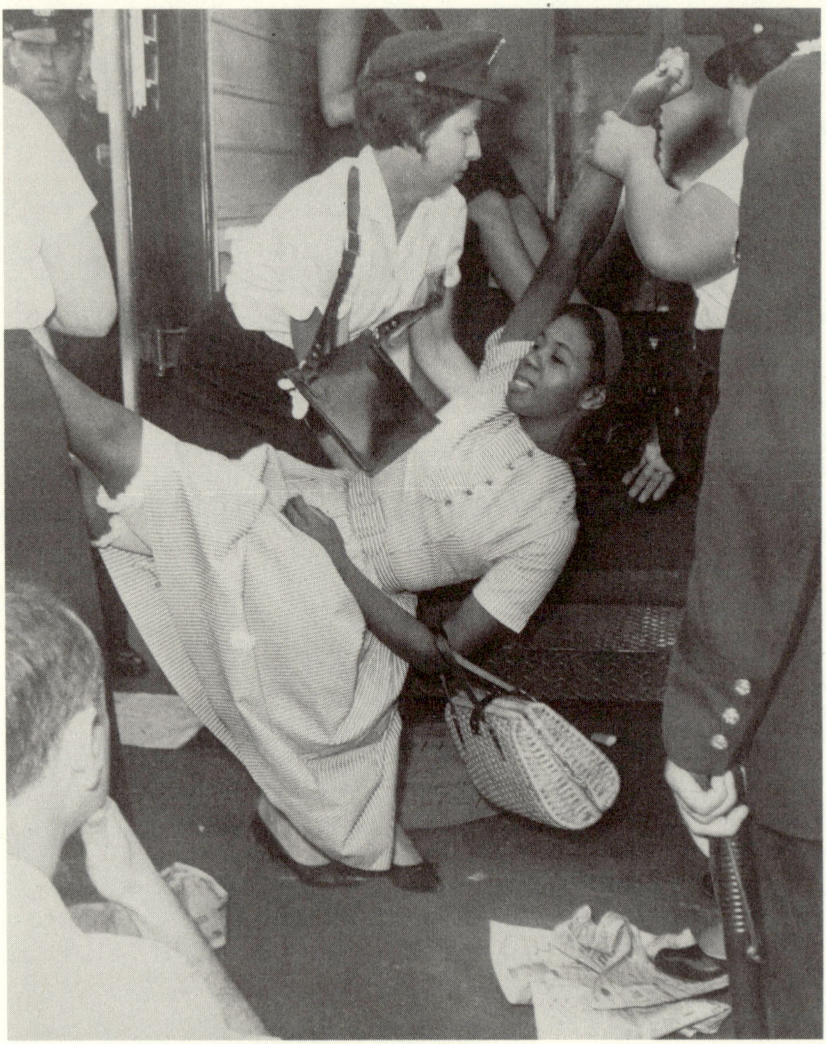

Songs My Mother Taught Me

Why the Artist Must Take Sides

SAUL WILLIAMS

Haymarket Books
Chicago, Illinois

Published in 2026 by
Haymarket Books
P.O. Box 180165
Chicago, IL 60618
www.haymarketbooks.org

Paperback ISBN: 979-8-88890-584-5
Hardcover ISBN: 979-8-88890-585-2
eBook ISBN: 979-8-88890-780-1

Distributed to the trade in the US through Consortium Book Sales and Distribution (www.cbsd.com) and internationally through Ingram Publisher Services International (www.ingramcontent.com).

This book was published with the generous support of Lannan Foundation, Wallace Action Fund, and Marguerite Casey Foundation.

Special discounts are available for bulk purchases by organizations and institutions. Please email info@haymarketbooks.org for more information.

Cover design by Thomas Colligan.
Cover image and frontispiece photograph by Dick DeMarsico. The author's mother, Juanita Sealy, Brooklyn, New York, 1963. Courtesy of the Library of Congress, Prints and Photographs Division.

Printed in Canada by union labor.

Library of Congress Cataloging-in-Publication data is available.
Library of Congress Control Number: 2026941410

10 9 8 7 6 5 4 3 2 1

FSC
www.fsc.org
MIX
Paper | Supporting responsible forestry
FSC® C103567

Contents

The Vanguard series illustrates the poet's power of persuasion in the arena of political struggle. Each of these brief books include a poem and a piece of nonfiction on art and politics by a writer impassioned by a single issue. Poets tackle subjects ranging from general strikes to independent bookstores as alternative learning spaces to offer answers to the perennial question "What does poetry have to do with politics?" This series offers answers, complexly and comprehensively, from some of today's most insightful, active, and talented poets.

A CALL TO ARMS

I had never seen
so many dead children.

Count on fingers.

Count toes.
Count sheep.
Count beats.
Count blessings.

The murders
they took no count of
is how I learned to count.

Learning to tell time
felt more like being told.

Counted the little hands
as big hands retrieved
the persistence of memory
from beneath the rubble.

The clock is a tank.

I saw a body bouquet
from beneath an armored car
and counted each blood-soaked flower.

Keeping time
is a quiet alignment.

The souls of martyrs
weave between drum patterns.

These rhythms
despite the times
cannot be programmed
nor can they be stopped.

Our chopped hands
a call to arms.

Western civilization
an artificial intelligence

yet our drums
have always
been wireless.

Songs my mother taught me
refuse their place in time.

They dance before
they walk
and think
outside the mind.

Songs my mother taught me
at any given time
will populate a mountainside
and teach me how to climb.

Songs my mother taught me
replace anthems and flags
and animate our body parts
from within plastic bags.

The weight of flesh
when torn apart
has weighed down
many poems

yet Mother's songs
come bearing arms
with drums to down the drones.

Introduction

After the revolutionary poet Amiri Baraka recited his poem "Somebody Blew Up America" following the targeted destruction of the World Trade Center on September 11, 2001, he was stripped of his New Jersey state poet laureateship and accused of antisemitism.* His poem, a long list of US state-sanctioned crimes against humanity, was mostly tolerable to state officials even as Baraka dabbled in conspiracy theory and questioned the origin of AIDS. However, his daring to suggest Israel's foreknowledge or involvement in a terrorist attack went too far, for far too many, in 2001. Conflating anti-Zionism with antisemitism, as the New Jersey governor did at the time, was the practice then as it is now. The state lauds or penalizes poets, so poetry must be powerful, but what is the weight of a poem?

* In fact, "the state government attempted to pass legislation that would allow the governor to formally remove Baraka but, unable to do so, decided to abolish the laureateship altogether." Michael Leong, "Amiri Baraka's Anti-Epic Poem About America's Destruction," *Lithub,* July 28, 2020.

The MK-84s supplied to Israel by the United States weigh two thousand pounds and vaporize any human beings within a four-hundred-yard (365-meter) radius, making it possible to murder and leave no trace. As of this writing, the US has transferred more than fourteen thousand of them to Israel since October 2023.[1] Are any poems as powerful? Yes, though the effect is not instant vaporization. Maybe the correct question is "Are poems as harmful as bombs?" Should we worry about poems falling into the wrong hands? Might these words be used against me? Will they bring harm to my family or yours? Might they narrate a means beyond unfathomable genocides, mercenaries, slave-like exploitation of workers, all somehow postulated for the progress of humanity? Might they stimulate mass movements?

It's ironic how, in the "progress" of technological advances, the West maintains its foothold on analog forms of exploitation, destabilization, and murder, as if the settler-colonial and imperial paradox within the racial-capitalist framework cannot escape genocide as a means of achieving its aims. But what does that have to do with poetry? With art? With music, theater, and dance? How should an artist respond? Should we simply be relegated to providing a much-needed relief from daily hardships and leave the heavy lifting to organizers, resistance fighters, and politicians? There are other ways that our creative work might be of service.

I remember memorizing Clay's monologue from Amiri Baraka's 1964 Obie Award–winning play, *Dutchman*, for a production at Spelman College in the early nineties. Every play we did in that theater was intended to heighten the consciousness of the student body. There was no such thing as art for art's sake. There was only ceremony and opportunity to uplift the voices of playwrights who had taken the time and energy to keep Black struggle and liberation front of mind. Theater was not only there to entertain or provoke. Theater also operated as a place for memorial and a means to deprogram and heal harms done through lived experience.

Dutchman is set on the New York City subway, where a middle-aged white woman attempts to seduce a young, three-button-suited Black dude. She weaves between flirt and insult before inviting him to dance on the crowded train car and loudly castigating him as an Uncle Tom when he will not. The young man, Clay, finally explodes, releasing his pent-up rage with a slap and craftily articulated Black fury. After Clay finishes his speech, while he grabs his bag to exit the train, the woman stabs him in the chest and calls on the other passengers on the train, who are colluding with her, to carry off and get rid of his body as she sets her eyes on another young Black man, who enters at the next stop.

Witnessing and participating in plays such as this vaporized any doubts I might have had about the power of art. Art at its most powerful forced us to interrogate the reality we Black students faced when we left the theater while freeing us from the rules and regimens of respectability. Baraka didn't need to be the poet laureate of New Jersey (the same state that held a bounty on Assata Shakur's head) in order to remain one of the most revered laureates of a generation of poets, playwrights, musicians, visual artists, and directors charged with the responsibility to uplift and empower through artwork to put us into motion to counteract the violent and systemic powers used against us. Their work, along with the work of previous generations of artists, scholars, and organizers has charged the fuck out of me.

This book came about because I could not shut up during the ongoing US-backed Israeli genocide against the Palestinian people. Although I took some pride in the few poets and artists who realized that their stages and platforms might hold some actual weight, far too many seemed to either lack the political education or the heart (a word that holds "art" in it) to connect the dots between entertainment, escape, and propaganda: cowboys as heroes, and cops and secret service men as dignified protagonists are not only selling tickets and popcorn, they're selling a settler-colonial myth. Some artists believe they have no place discussing politics, or, at least, politics beyond their scope. Yet a live-streamed genocide should bring everything into question. A question that becomes: What role can you play? What is within your power to help bring it to an end? Do you need to be a politician? Do people hold power over politicians? Is there a way to help inspire people? Are people inspired by art, by information, by the actions of other people? Or, if art influences culture, and genocide is a part of—or is being introduced into—the culture, can art be likened to an immune system, there to fight the invasion of a deadly virus? Would a healthy culture have a stronger immune system? If artists flag the virus, are they doing their job? Who knows? I exited my comfort zone and posted thoughts and poems, those that would normally sit marinating in notebooks, as they occurred. I even addressed some of them to the president, on my Twitter page. It felt more crucial to signal to people crying out to be seen that we see them than to wait for the perfect sentence.

When politicians and media corroborate the lies of the state, people who hold no office are left to distinguish information from misinformation. Social media platforms are complicit in trying to hide or divert attention away from crimes happening right before our eyes. In terms of social media, learning to sift out misinformation has had less to do with research and more to do with reading between lines and fishing out real stories from Palestinian voices and perspectives rather than paying any mind to what the white boys at the *Times* have to say, or the White House for that matter. From writing my poem "Coltan as Cotton" for the film *Neptune Frost (Martyr Loser King),* a process that made me into an investigative poet, I actively started to disrupt an algorithm aimed at denial and erasure.

In *Neptune Frost* there is a song called "Fuck Mr. Google," written by one of the lead actors, Bertrand "Kaya Free" Nintereste. Kaya Free wrote it after learning that big tech companies' reliance on cheap resources imposes standards of cheap labor, enforced by violence and lobbying, and is used as an excuse and means to destabilize governments, while ensuring slave-like conditions for new generations in the rare earth–mineral mines of countries like his, Burundi, and, of course, the Democratic Republic of Congo (DRC). A year after the film's release, we learned about those minerals being weaponized by Google, Amazon, Microsoft, and other companies involved in the surveillance and weapons technology used to target and kill Palestinians. This same technology later showed up at weapons conventions as "field tested."[2] What means of communication could be used to convey that genocide was not an aberration of the system but a function of the system itself? The link is in the parallel between a technological "operating system" and the way a settler-colonial system operates.

Genocide is a function of the settler-colonial system; the system's technology is being used to enforce it.

Propagandized kids of settler states and the West, who've been taught they live in the most powerful "democracy," "the most liberal democracy," "the land of the free," or that they are "chosen" and therefore worth more than those who are not, have a lot in common: Black death and Indigenous erasure. But if teachers are punished for teaching about genocide, the journalists forbidden—or, if they're Palestinian, killed—for reporting it, while politicians actively support it, then, like the poem Assata Shakur wrote right before she escaped from her New Jersey prison cell asks, "What is left?"[3]

That the "American Dream" is a settler-colonial myth is a hard lesson to teach in a system that indoctrinates its citizens, from classrooms to cartoons to movies to media that all maintain an American exceptionalist narrative. It may not be the role of the artist to stand in for the teacher—which many rappers, as an example, did do during hip-hop's golden age—yet, as Baraka insisted, we must "raise the level of our understanding of the world so that we understand . . . why it acts the way it does. So that we know who are our friends and who are our enemies. And right now, so that we build that united front. What is the artist's job? To make war. The artist's job is unrelenting war on evil."[4]

As a poet, the page is a stage. Both are tools for learning and unlearning. The words perform in our mind. In February 2025, when I asked Maya Marshall, a poet in her own right and now my editor at Haymarket, what kind of literary submission she would like from me, I was looking for direction, an assignment from a publisher whose overall output I found admirable and important in its support of writers and academics on the left and in publishing on Palestine. I appreciate a publisher whose literary work also challenges the haunt of the CIA's subtly planted purpose of US MFA creative writing programs, as helmed by the Iowa Writer's Workshop in the 1930s. At that time, as part of the culture war against Communism, the goal was to shift American literature away from a populist direction—to contain the US political and cultural climate by streamlining certain values into an acceptable canon of what was to be praised and published. "Good literature, students learned, contains 'sensations, not doctrines; experiences, not dogmas; memories, not philosophies.'"[5] Abstract Expressionism over principled anticapitalism. These efforts naturally spilled over into journalism and partially explain the US media class that holds up outlets like *The New York Times* as a high point of excellence in the craft and of careerist ambition, even as "the paper of record" has used its leverage and position to very openly (and criminally) manufacture consent for—and, as has been publicly documented, attempt to whitewash—genocide.

Maya asked how I see the relationship between politics and art and cited an interest in the poet's perspective. She had listened to a speech I delivered the previous November, just before the 2024 US presidential election, at the "End of Empire and the Future of Freedom" conference at the University of Santa Barbara. She asked if I would consider expanding or writing essays to accompany the publication of that speech, which was focused on reminding folks of the power they had when and if they withheld their labor—in other words, a general strike. In that speech (chapter 8 of this book), I called for a general strike and pointed out that people might fairly say to me, "Well, Saul, you're a poet—what kind of labor can you withhold?" Following Maya Angelou's guiding statement for critique, "Anything an artist writes should be written with the urgency of what they would write if someone were holding a gun in their mouth," I take her notion as a wonderful point of interrogation for any poem. Could these be my last words? It is this seriousness with which I take poetry that drew in my editor. We agreed that additional reflections and analysis could cover the broader subjects of art and politics.

This book is my response to her query and to questions I've posed to myself as to why my personal relationship to art and politics is so tightly bound.

When speaking about this book to friends, I say that it reads like a memoir, but a memoir focused mostly on just three years of my life—that is, on my political education and its application. The book that follows is my exploration of how decisions I made in the third grade—to be an actor and to be an exchange student—helped shape who I am today.

Another way of phrasing this query would be "What radicalized you?" Of course, the etymological roots of the word "radical" mean just that: roots. My roots are in a New York household belonging to parents who resisted the state so that I could have the rights I've enjoyed. That my art is rooted in a politic feels more like a mere observation of all art than a personal confession, similar to the acknowledgment that an algorithmic operating system carries the political persuasion of the—in most cases—men who program them.[6]

That art can serve as propaganda and not simply as a weather vane indicating which direction the wind blows—that art also can, and must, exist within an understanding that there are forces aimed at controlling the wind, thus art must be armed to sometimes work against the wind—is as embedded into the role of the artist as are the considerations of weight and stability in the practice of a carpenter. It cannot be reduced to being true to one's craft any more than Muhammad Ali's refusing to fight in Vietnam can be interpreted as his being true to boxing, or to his title. Rather, it was his unwillingness to betray his own principles or his love for his people.

A deep-seated love of humanity lies in the heart of every revolutionary. Those who are willing to put their love and their lives on the line at the risk of sounding stupid, being laughed at, hitting the wrong note, being rejected or even martyred are not acting merely as functionaries of a system. Sometimes the work pushes up against the system itself.

Baraka's work reminds us that art is dangerous because it can charge us to counteract the power structures that oppress us. When he passed at the age of seventy-nine, in January 2014, I was asked to read a poem at his funeral, as he lay in state in Newark, New Jersey. Here is what I read:

This NGH died for something.
I don't go for old age.
I don't go for disease.
I say murder.
Which poets die from natural causes?
Which poems kill?
I saw the rifles pointed.
Jesse Jackson with that blood on his shirt.
BarakaBarakaBarakaBaraka
Pitbull orchestra.
Rottweiler choir.

Charlie Parker, what you say?
Amiri Baraka was no centrist
unless u count right between the eyes.
Pianos make better sense of trees
than the trees themselves.
Monk on an "expression-scriber"
A typewriter is corny!
Washington uncross the Delaware.
Tell the governor
to stop up the bridge.
We can't let
this poet's spirit
get out of here.
This is a stick-up.
Amiri, get out of the coffin.
I saw you dancing on Langston's ashes.
They raised the bounty
on Assata Shakur's head
and called it "inflation."
Lying in state
in the state of New Jersey.
American culture is televisional.
You can't go out like that.
Time to conceptualize a series.
The good news is
half of America was
waiting for u to die
so they could read u.

They done Loku'd
the twitterverse.
Either this is a funeral
or this is the senate floor.
We all knew the politicians would show up.
Somebody said
Jesus got stuck
at the border.
I say,
Amiri, get up and walk.

Chapter One

In Terms of Culture, Shit, We Were Rich

When my friend, Kiini, told me she grew up in a culturally middle-class family, naturally, I asked her what she meant. "We had quite a few seasons on government cheese, but walls covered in art and books. Music of every genre. Live music. Expansive philosophical principles. . . ." In my case, those principles and the conversations around them included what some would call Black "radical" politics and early exposure to the poetry of Amiri Baraka, Sonia Sanchez, Nikki Giovanni, Larry Neal, Langston Hughes, Zora Neale Hurston, the Black Arts Movement, political theater, gospel concerts, double Dutch contests. . . . In terms of culture, shit, we were rich.

I was raised in Newburgh, New York. My mother, born and raised in East New York, Brooklyn, was an elementary school teacher. My father, from Brownsville, Brooklyn, was the pastor of a Baptist church, though he had trained to sing opera at New York's School of

Music and Art as a teen. They both became active in the civil rights movement as young adults. There's a widely circulated photo of my mother being carried by the NYPD into a patrol wagon for protesting that the city hire Black construction workers, which was on the front page of the *New York Herald Tribune* in 1963. There's footage of my dad participating in protests in South Carolina in the early sixties. Their views were consistent with the "troublemakers" and "rabble-rousers" of their times. Proud Black church folks working primarily in the Northern landscape of the movement. Children of the early forties, who did not become Panthers or join any of the more radical organizations of the late sixties and early seventies, but absolutely never had a disparaging word to say against them—celebrating every triumph, mourning every loss, standing against every injustice, standing for the wrongly prosecuted, and, subsequently, standing for every political prisoner.

Their lives were peopled with activists, church folk, and members of the community providing mutual aid through childcare, free meals, showing up to speak out, creating youth organizations to keep kids off the street, while also interacting with the many elements of the street. At one point, my father's church was literally between a crack house and a brothel. Everybody knew and spoke to each other.

Sometimes my dad would throw in a little "Am I gonna see you in church this Sunday?" And occasionally, particularly on holidays, you'd catch the brothel workers or the drug-kingpin son of a church member squeezed into the pews for Sunday service.

Newburgh was many things at once. Sitting on the Hudson River, just sixty miles north of New York City, it was a weekend destination of the Fifth Avenue elite during the Gilded Age. George Washington himself had been headquartered there during the last eighteen months of the Revolutionary War, in a building that was the first site to be acquired and preserved by any US state as "historic." It was at this site that Washington swayed a tired and unpaid Continental Army on the verge of mutiny, which would have meant a military coup in the early years of America's forming, with his renowned Newburgh Address. Andrew Jackson Downing, considered the father of US landscape architecture, who argued for the construction of New York City's Central Park, was born in Newburgh, and its central park bears his name. Ironically, the construction of Central Park displaced a thriving community of freed Black American landowners, known as Seneca Village. If you imagine that population displaced into the city of Newburgh, you'll have a taste of the city I grew up in. Old buildings and old souls.

In my case, the old building was the house I grew up in. It was built by the infamous architect Stanford

White in 1906, the year of his murder and the subsequent "Trial of the Century," at which the who's who of New York elite would testify as witnesses to his murder, front row, opening night of *Mam'zelle Champagne*, in what was then his most popular building, Madison Square Garden. By the time my parents arrived in Newburgh, I was one year old, and Newburgh had gone from being the nation's first electric city, with Edison's first power plant, to a city that was majority Black and ever distant from the question of power.

My father originally pastored an old Baptist church named Ebenezer, with a parsonage, where we lived, beside it; then he founded a new church down the street, called Baptist Temple, when the old folks at Ebenezer decided they preferred traditional hymns over a gospel choir. The new church had no parsonage, so, in 1977, my parents took out a loan and purchased a six-thousand-square-foot Victorian home for thirty thousand dollars. Only problem was they couldn't always afford to heat it in the winter. I remember my mother putting my jeans in the oven before waking us up for school, like "Rise and shine. Your clothes are nice and warm."

My dad's church was made up of poor and working-class Black Americans, many from the South, some from the Caribbean, all carrying on and being fed by the tradition of the church as a touchstone of the community's spiritual and political health. I never laughed harder, some never prayed harder; old ladies caught the Holy Ghost while the choir sang the latest renditions of praise songs. Ushers in white gloves, fried chicken in the basement, "Ms. Bowie made a sweet potato pie for Pastor and now we having sweet potato pie for breakfast."

A friend and neighbor would occasionally show up at my father's church with his guitar, and my dad would unswervingly invite him into the pulpit to lead the church in a few songs. I remember thinking something along the lines of "Why is it that anytime this white mf show up in this Black-ass church, with its banging choir, does my dad invite this old man to lead us in school songs like 'Kumbayah,' 'If I Had a Hammer,' or 'This Land Is Your Land'?" When I finally asked my parents what the deal was, they were like, "Well, Pete helped popularize and even wrote some of those songs."* I remember another singer, named Odetta, staying at our house and being a guest soloist with our church choir at the county fair, where she purchased a wicker-framed oval mirror that she gifted us. It overlooked the bench where we threw our coats after school every day. As the pastor of a midsized Black church, my dad would often get sent free tickets to any and every Black play—or play with Black

* Now that I think about it, growing up with Pete Seeger might explain why my first ventures into songwriting were attempts at writing songs for the school chorus.

actors—on or off-Broadway in hopes that he might return, as we often did, with a busload of church folks. Ntozake Shange, Charles Fuller, Athol Fugard, August Wilson, Lorraine Hansberry, *The Wiz*, *Your Arms Too Short to Box with God*, you name it.

We never went to school on Dr. King's birthday. Long before it was a federal holiday, we sat in packed churches reciting poems, singing songs, and having Black History Quiz Bowls: Who invented the traffic light? The gas mask? The blood bank? Who was the first nigga at the North Pole? Who can name all the countries in Africa? Who is Frantz Fanon? What was the "Negritude" movement? When was the Harlem Renaissance? All this, coupled with the in-your-face politics of early hip-hop, laid the backdrop of my upbringing. We ain't had no money, but we were deep-steeped in culture. So, yeah, "culturally middle-class," with a discerning gaze on whiteness—even if my over-corrected grammar and enunciation had some peers saying I talked like a white boy, while white folks unfailingly (failingly) commented on how articulate I was. The dichotomy between "insult" and "compliment" kept me fixated on colonial imprints, remnants of slavery, which gave me the retorts I needed when kids just a few shades lighter than me might tease me for being too dark: "Why are you bragging about the fact that your great-grandmother was raped by her slave-master?" I learned early that a firm grasp on history and politics would keep me sharp. Still, when I pinpoint a moment that lit my particular path, I think on the moment when I decided what that path would be.

I attended third grade at a magnet school called Horizons on the Hudson. We had regular classes in the morning, but in the afternoon we could choose from dozens of "options and electives." The electives were educational: you could study a particular field of history, science, a language. The "options" were games, sports, hobbies. I chose a class called "Shake Hands with Shakespeare," where we would get to perform in a school play. Beyond us sitting around a table, taking turns reading the play aloud, I don't remember actually auditioning, but somehow I was cast as Marc Antony in *Julius Caesar.* I remember borrowing my older sister's acid-wash purple mini-skirt, oversized belt, and silver slouchy boots for the performance. "If you have tears, prepare to shed them now. . ." I loved the pointed economy of the language and how it danced off the tongue. I loved the process, the time we spent sitting around the table deciphering layers of meaning, political and social climates, always in terms of "beats" and "objectives." I loved the study of character, backstory, physical, philosophic, and psychological dispositions. I loved the ritual of embodiment and its fluidity, once the text was committed to memory; the active engagement of the other actors, all with their own emotional arcs and journeys. I felt so thoroughly stimulated and connected that one day I came home from rehearsal and announced at the dinner table, "I want to be an actor when I grow up."

My father, who had not only studied opera but also, when he was in third grade, sung as a regular on an NBC show of the early fifties called *Star Time Kids*, had an immediate response, "I'll support you as an actor if you get a law degree." Now why this nigga thought this way, go figure. He had been "called to preach" as a young man before venturing too deeply into an artistic career as an adult. I suppose he simply envisioned my having a more "stable" life than many of the artists he knew and loved. Yet, my mother, who spoke freely about the actors she very openly adored, had an immediate response to my father's reply that clarified a path and perspective for me that grows frighteningly more relevant to this day. What she said was, "Oh, then you should do your next school report on Paul Robeson. He was an actor and a lawyer."

Chapter Two

The Artist Must Take Sides

Paul Robeson was an actor, singer, lawyer, athlete, and outspoken advocate for human rights, workers' rights, and the rights of African and Indigenous people on the continent, in the United States, and throughout the world. Born in 1898 in Princeton, New Jersey, he was the son of a schoolteacher mother and a preacher father, who had escaped from the Roberson* plantation in North Carolina via the Underground Railroad, arriving in Philadelphia in 1860. While in high school, where he excelled in sports (and performed in *Julius Caesar*), Paul won a statewide academic competition for a scholarship to Rutgers University, which he would attend after becoming his high school's valedictorian. In 1915, Robeson was the third African American to attend Rutgers, and he led the school's football, track, field, and speech-and-debate teams while also singing in the glee club and at small clubs in town for extra

* "Roberson" was the name of the family that enslaved them; the Robesons changed the spelling of the name.

money. In 1919, he graduated from Rutgers Phi Beta Kappa and was, once again, valedictorian of his class. He then paid his way through Columbia Law School by accepting singing engagements and playing professional football for the NFL on the weekends. For me, Paul Robeson was a blueprint.

While at Columbia Law, Paul met and married another trailblazer, chemist-turned-anthropologist, author, and advocate for African independence and Pan-Africanism Eslanda Goode. Eslanda not only managed and helped fashion Robeson's singing and acting career to worldwide acclaim, but she also, through her own political curiosity,* deepened his politics to the point that he became actively outspoken on anticolonialism and anti-imperialism. This collaborative political education would later explain how someone who was once celebrated as the shining star of the

* Eslanda entered the anthropology department of London School of Economics in 1933, while the Robesons lived in London. There she became close friends with her classmate Jomo Kenyatta, who introduced her into the community of young Anglophone and Francophone African anticolonialists. During this time, she was also pen pals with her close friend Zora Neale Hurston. She maintained a strong critique of the colonial ideologies within the anthropological field and was determined to travel the continent to write a book that did not center African people as "primitive." Her book *African Journey* was released in 1945, dedicated to "the brothers and sisters who will know what I mean."

American stage and cinema, featured in concert halls worldwide, would eventually die in relative obscurity for future generations.

My first report on Robeson focused greatly on his triumphs, the long list of accomplishments and Black firsts, the number of languages he sang in, yet it was impossible not to learn of his solidarity with trade unionists, miners, and everyday workers, as well as his assertion that "the artist must take sides" as he sang for soldiers on the front lines during the Spanish Civil War, standing firmly against the rise of fascism in the 1930s. (Rumor has it that while he sang on those front lines, absolutely no shots were fired, as soldiers from both sides clamored to hear his voice.) In this same time period, he also spoke at great length about the need for an independent cinema that did not reinforce negative racial stereotypes or spread Western propaganda—yes, in the 1930s. Writing that report as a third grader was my first time having to look up "propaganda" and "fascism" or think about "independent cinema" and contemplate what they might have to do with each other.

At nine, I was already familiar with the projection of stereotypes in film and television, though my awareness didn't stop me from enjoying reruns of *The Little Rascals* despite its racist depictions of Black children like Buckwheat and Stymie. The show seemed to be a study in class, privilege, and solidarity—the old-fashioned black-and-white footage had the feeling of an archive, and the children all had each other's backs (except for sometimes Alfalfa). I used to stay up late with my father to watch reruns of *The Honeymooners.* Occasionally, an episode of *Amos 'n' Andy* or a reference to it would slip through the cracks, and what was nostalgic for my dad was, for me, proof and testimony of our existence, in black and white. I recognized the people just as surely as I recognized the stereotypes enmeshed in a performance of Blackness that served as a marker of what was demanded by US society and a testament of how far we had come.

Both *The Honeymooners* and *Amos 'n' Andy* began as radio shows in the 1920s. *Amos 'n' Andy* held the distinction of having been a radio minstrel show voiced and created by white actors* for the entertainment of white listeners, who gut-laughed at the heavily exaggerated drawl of white actors in linguistic Blackface in sketches that depicted the childlike naïveté and feather-brained get-rich-quick schemes in the far-fetched Black life of the white American imagination. In the 1950s, when it was fashioned into a television show for CBS, the producers decided to hire Black actors, and thus *Amos 'n' Andy* became the first US television show with an all-Black cast. I had also seen

* Freeman Gosden and Charles Correll.

my share of Shirley Temple films where she was sometimes accompanied by Bojangles or Stepin Fetchit.

It should hardly shock that Paul Robeson spoke in the 1930s about racial stereotypes in Hollywood and the need for an independent cinema. Just fifteen years earlier, when he was seventeen, the first major US-made feature film to loom over American culture was *Birth of a Nation*, whose portrayal of African Americans—white actors in blackface cast as dim-witted delinquents bent on sexually dominating white women—helped spur the rebirth of the Ku Klux Klan as the supposed saviors of the "white race," and especially of white womanhood. I mean, if we're looking at the role of cinema or art in not only perpetuating stereotypes but also serving as propaganda to literally stir misdirected men into action, why not start at the first mf blockbuster?*

What I understood at my young age was that our status in the Western world was evolving. That we were

---

* "Moving pictures appear at that juncture when a new racial regime was being stitched together from remnants of its predecessors and new cloth accommodating the disposal of immigrants, colonial subjects, and insurgencies among the native poor. With the first attempts at composing a national identity in disarray, a new whiteness became the basis for the reintegration of American society." Cedric Robinson, *In Forgeries of Memory and Meaning: Blacks and the Regimes of Race in American Theater and Film Before World War II* (University of North Carolina Press, 2007).

a part of a struggle. That each generation was experiencing newer "freedoms." I was probably giving white people more benefit of the doubt than I do today, yet at the age of eight or nine I was already clear on the fact that my parents had recently fought for rights that I was experiencing and that art was part of that movement and played a role in that struggle. My mother had told us proudly of the exuberance she had felt, driving through the streets of New York in the first car her modest teaching salary afforded her, a convertible Volkswagen Bug, with a huge Afro wig, blasting and singing along with James Brown's "Say It Loud—I'm Black and I'm Proud."

I understood that pride had forcibly been stripped from us. My complexion, coupled with my sensitivity, had privied me to the spectrum of discourse that went from "chocolatey" to "frying pan" and "burnt toast"—the self-hate that took proportionate shape when colonial violence was internalized. My mother, whose only prayer after birthing my two older sisters was for a "dark, dark boy with curly, curly hair," had called me by middle name, Stacey, since birth. As a result, I had naturally acquired a nickname that I was called whenever I wasn't around or one assumed I wasn't in hearing distance. I would be at a friend's house, playing after school, and some other kid might call my friend to ask what they were up to, and the response was always, "I'm here playing with Stacey." *Pause.* "Uh-huh." That pause was the perpetual (and unnecessary, for there weren't that many Staceys in our community) point of clarification: "Black Stacey?" "Uh-huh." I never perceived it as in insult, just one of my many points of observation. What I was observing was a generation that had inherited a struggle from the complete dehumanization of chattel slavery to Emancipation, Reconstruction, the Harlem Renaissance, the civil rights movement, and the Black Power and Black Arts movements, slowly digesting the lessons yet highly subject to the impressions left by years of paper-bag tests and misplaced associations of beauty and savagery. But wait, here was Paul Robeson, dark like me.

I think it's fair to say that one of my points of connection with Robeson was the fact that he was dark like my mother's favorite actor, Sidney Poitier. Being born with a complexion that was constantly commented on, that singled me out, certainly had its effects. I was made to be overly conscious of my skin tone, and if I were to achieve "pride," external confirmations of my potential beauty or intelligence were necessary. I was also highly sensitive to language. "Black and Ugly." "Black and Evil." "Dark Days." "Black Tuesday." It seemed that everything evil, sinister, unfortunate, or ugly was more readily understood if the word "Black" or "Dark" was placed before it. Black Americans from my grandmother's generation would refer to themselves as "Negro" or "Colored." Words like "African" and "Black" carried the weight of years of negative portrayals and systemic abuses, yet Black Pride and Black Power were pushing a younger generation to embrace their Blackness, their natural hair, the "Afro," even going so far as to flip the most hateful term that had been used against us to a term of endearment. I wasn't allowed to use the word "nigger," or "nigga," growing up, but I loved the way my father and folks around me let it fall off their tongues. I would sometimes, in the middle of the night, head to the kitchen to get something to drink and find my father sitting alone in front of the television. The way he'd look up, smile, and say, "Hey, little nigga," felt like a hug. Yet there was another term, one I was unfamiliar with, that I was forced to look up for that first report on Robeson: "blacklisted."

Chapter Three

Freedom Ain't Free

Had I considered that art could get you killed, imprisoned, or restricted from traveling or performing? That you might be brought before a judge or Congress to explain what you meant when you sang that song? That there were ideas to be extracted from art where the listener or viewer might walk away with an altered viewpoint, one that might encourage them to break the law or, God forbid, counter the foreign policy of their country? Did I understand that a work of art might serve as an act of treason?

That an artist could be used as an example? That they might be made to answer for their beliefs or thoughts if they ran counter to whatever authority, beyond audience, might police art?

These ideas ran counter to the merits that I had been made to believe, on school grounds at least, laid the groundwork for the country I was being raised in. The constant declarations of "freedom" under the weight of the Black experience were enough for me to understand the glaring inconsistencies that predicated that I would have no toy guns, due to how police were prone to target Black boys, or how I would be given "the talk," which my mother had already delivered by the time I was in third grade, along with an added "And if you ever get drafted, we will drive right up to Canada. No son of mine will ever fight for this country."

I ain't learn shit about patriotism growing up except to watch my back around the mfs who practiced it. My grandfather, uncles, and cousins on my mother's side had all been in the service, but wasn't nobody joining for love of country. They had either been drafted or seeking a way out of poverty, a possibility of stability. We lived in defiance of what the ruling class of the country stood for, constantly demanding that it assumed the responsibilities of securing and upholding the freedoms that it pronounced outwardly. My parents had been arrested for rights I now took for granted, rights that, according to the US Constitution, should not have had to be fought for—still, that wasn't art; that was protest. I knew plenty of protest songs or songs that had been sung at protests, songs that accompanied movements, but I had never considered singers being arrested, stripped by the state of their right to travel or perform. That Robeson found himself in this position was a confirmation of the inbred hypocrisy that we understood to be a given in the American system. That he faced these circumstances under the suspicion of being a Communist sent me back to the dictionary. What was so wrong with being a Communist?

Growing up under the subversive effects of US propaganda, it was clear that Communism was something I wasn't supposed to like, but I didn't really know why. At that age, it wasn't from lessons from my parents or necessarily from my teachers. Yet, it was definitely from the subtext of films and television shows, from the punchlines of cartoons and comics, that I had somehow acquired the sense that Communism was something that stood opposed to American "freedom." That word was paired mostly, it seemed, with the "free market" and our supposed right to free speech, but on the ground, we were clearly still fighting for ours, and, although incremental advances had been made, there was a very visible line of demarcation between the written law and the lived experience. The US "founding fathers" had written, "All men are created equal," while owning slaves. The hypocrisy of American freedom outshined any rockets' red glare. Yet, we watched the Olympics and heard stories of athletes defecting from the Soviet Union, given the impression by commentators that Soviet athletes were forced to train from a young age at gunpoint and stood on long lines for food. There was no nuance in American propaganda as related to its Cold War efforts to turn impressionable minds against Communism and socialism. No explanations were given beyond the idea that citizens of these countries lived under authoritarian regimes and experienced "lesser freedoms," while we folks maintained burning questions about the rising cost of education and the big deal made of the fact that my mother's job as a teacher meant that my father, sisters, and I were afforded healthcare coverage under her plan, when most in our community simply didn't have insurance.

Governmental, systemic, and corporate injustices were glaringly apparent in our daily lives and in our community, as was wealth disparity. Places like my father's church provided a level of mutual aid and assistance that stepped up where the government fell short. Yet, in that first exposure to Paul Robeson and the question of Communism, I may have subconsciously held on to the idea that he had been wrongly accused rather than the precept that he should have every right to be a Communist, and, if he was one, it was probably for a damn good reason. Through reading his speeches and embracing his outlook on a world of injustices that the poor, working, and disenfranchised faced in a capitalist economy that aimed to exploit them rather than share the wealth of production, I was being coaxed into questioning the indoctrination inherent in my American upbringing.

Coincidently, this was the same age that I began questioning my religious indoctrination. My father had preached that "only through accepting Christ as your savior" could one be accepted into heaven. Yet, we were also taught that Christ was the embodiment of love; thus, it followed, in my mind at least, that by accepting "love" as your savior you should be good to go. I had reflected on this because a girl in my third-grade class was simply one of the nicest people I had ever met. I had seen her share her snack and lunch with kids who had forgotten theirs or didn't bring money to purchase it. She let kids copy her homework before class or would help those who needed it over her lunch break. This generosity of hers struck me as a real kindness. She never complained or made anyone feel bad; thus, in an environment that had its share of bullies, she was quietly respected.

This was not a popular girl. Aside from her being in my class, I think I noticed her because she was regularly dipped in Benetton and Izod, the preppy white-girl fashion trend that was starting to catch my eye. But another thing I learned about her, which wasn't a big deal, was that she was Jewish, as were many other kids in my class. So, one day, I began to tell my family about this girl, how nice she was, how she seemed to exemplify a loving-kindness that, in my short-lived experience, seemed "Christ-like." "But," I added, taking the question to my father, "she's born into a Jewish family. Is she going to hell?" My dad had a kind of remote response: "Not if she accepts the Lord Jesus Christ as her savior." Unfortunately, my mom didn't follow up this time with "Well, you should do your next school report on . . ." It was clear to me that something was being gravely overlooked. There was no way that the happenstance of birth would damn one to hell for not being a Christian. Clearly, one could be loving and an embodiment of love without needing to encounter someone who tells you the story of a kid from Nazareth. It was his message they were trying to implant in us, so why fixate on the need of accepting "the Lord Jesus Christ" as your savior? Couldn't you simply accept love?

I can't say I wrestled with this question. I innately understood my father's position to be shortsighted and proof of a religious rigidity that would act against the spiritual teachings that were themselves more supple and aligned with nature than a dude saying, "This is the only way!" Would God behave like those McCarthyite senators who questioned Robeson, fixated on heavily regulated formalities in which one wrong word would damn you to prison or hell? Would this God damn all Muslims, Jews, Buddhists, spiritualists, and nonreligious folks who happened to be born into non-Christian families in, possibly, non-Christian parts of the world, even if their moral sense and behavior were aligned with the teachings of Jesus? It just didn't sit right with me, and although it may have taken me a few years to articulate it, I felt clearly then that my father was mistaken for *blacklisting* my little classmate to the supposed fires of hell.*

---

* This reminds me of the time I thought that I was certain to be blacklisted in Hollywood for having to explain to a reputable casting agent why I was refusing to play a part that had been offered in a Black celebrity–laced dramatized audio recording of the Bible in the mid-2000s. Big names had agreed to read certain roles—I would be in A-list company, the casting agent assured me. Yet, this was in the midst of the US Global War on Terror, when it was relentlessly bombing and destroying the livelihoods of millions of Iraqis and Afghanis and openly discriminating through a manufactured paranoia against Arabs within its borders. The media, the airports, our daily lives had been rampant with Islamophobia since 9/11 (certainly before then as well), and it was clear that, like Communism, Islam—but more particularly anti-Arab hate—was carefully baked into films, in which portrayals of the distrustful, conniving, backward, or plain evil "terrorist" were reserved for Arab or Arab-looking actors. After 9/11, anti-Arab propaganda had reached a fever pitch, even though it felt pretty openly understood that the US was fighting on behalf of its interest in oil. I remember contemplating Kanye West's release of "Jesus Walks" at the beginning of the war. I was aware of the fact that soldiers are often listening to music in tanks and airplanes. The irony of them sometimes blasting groups like Rage Against the Machine while carrying out imperial orders was balanced by those who said they had begun to come to their senses through music that questioned the war and the role of empire. Yet, a hard-hitting Christian anthem like "Jesus Walks" could certainly lighten the load of a US soldier mercilessly bombing Muslims in the Middle East.

While researching Robeson's blacklisting for my report, I was surprised to come across news clips of a riot just a few miles down the road from Newburgh. The Peekskill Riots occurred when Robeson had been asked to headline a benefit concert for the Civil Rights Congress CRC in August 1949. The CRC, an organization headed by another African American attorney and close friend of the Robesons, William Patterson, had a similar mission to the NAACP with a wider scope.

I tried my best to explain to the casting agent that, although I had grown up in a Baptist church, I believed it was important that we wean ourselves from any form of religious fundamentalism, and that participating in a contemporary reading of the Bible worked counter to the direction in which I felt we needed to be heading. I told her I felt that religion offered a sometimes necessary crutch to help one stand upright in their understanding of nature, humanity, love, community, and service. Yet, it was also important—as you would know if you've ever broken an arm or leg—to at one point remove the cast and attempt to walk without the crutch. A physician would tell you that this step is crucial for rebuilding the musculature necessary to walk on your own. And pushing Christian propaganda at a time when the US was using religion to manufacture consent to kill millions of Muslims felt a little reckless. I was kind as could be, but I couldn't help thinking, "This woman will never cast me for nothing." My cover was blown. I can't say that I was ever officially blacklisted; as an actor it's difficult to determine why you don't get calls. But I couldn't help feeling that I had crossed a line by openly admitting that, despite my upbringing, I did not identify as Christian.

They intervened on behalf of Black families in cases of police brutality, white mob violence, unjust sentencing, and cases of discrimination and persecution on behalf of radicals, anarchists, and Communists. The April before the concert, Robeson delivered a speech at the World Congress for Peace, in Paris. The conference was sponsored by Cominform, a Soviet-funded coordinating body of Communist and workers' parties across Europe. The US was paying close attention.

This was the beginning of the Cold War between the US and the USSR, which would last until 1991 and began the witch hunt in the domestic United States known as the Red Scare. It would later be popularly referenced as "McCarthyism," after Wisconsin Republican senator Joseph McCarthy. Robeson, as a world-renowned figure who sang Negro spirituals, popular work songs—songs of workers—from around the world, and songs of national battles against fascism, was under close watch. He had already made connections between African liberation and anti-imperialism and shown sympathy for the Chinese during the Second Sino-Japanese War.

In 1940, he had met Chinese journalist and songwriter Liu Liangmo, who helped invent a new genre of Chinese fighting and folk songs that sparked a mass singing movement throughout China for war mobilization. Together, they recorded the 1941 album, *Chee Lai! Songs of New China*, with Robeson singing Liu's songs in Mandarin and English. Robeson loved the title song, "Chee Lai!" whose opening lyrics, translated, were "Arise, ye who refuse to bond slaves!," and it became a huge hit in China and across the world, with even the US Army Air Force Orchestra recording it for the opening and closing credits of the film *Why We Fight: The Battle of China* (1944), produced by the US State Department.* "Chee Lai!," also known as "The March of Volunteers," became a staple of Robeson's concerts for almost a decade and then became the national anthem of the newly formed People's Republic of China in 1949—the same year that Robeson appeared at the World Congress for Peace in Paris, along with his friend, the renowned African American sociologist and Pan-Africanist, W. E. B. Du Bois.

Before Robeson even began speaking, the Associated Press published a fabricated transcript of his speech, reporting that he had said the following:

> We colonial peoples have contributed to the building of the United States and are determined to share its wealth. We denounce the policy of the United States government which is similar to Hitler and Goebbels. It is unthinkable that American Negros would go to war on behalf of those who have oppressed us for generations against the

---

* *Why We Fight* was directed by Frank Capra.

> Soviet Union which in one generation has lifted our people to full human dignity.[1]

What he actually said was this:

> We in America do not forget that it is on the backs of the poor whites of Europe . . . and on the backs of millions of Black people the wealth of America has been acquired. And we are resolved that it shall be distributed in an equitable manner among all of our children and we don't want any hysterical stupidity about our participating in a war against anybody no matter whom. Our will to fight for peace is strong. We shall not make war on anyone. We shall not make war on the Soviet Union. We oppose those who wish to build up imperialist Germany and to establish fascism in Greece. We wish peace with Franco's Spain despite her fascism. We shall support peace and friendship among all nations, with Soviet Russia and the People's republics.[2]

The sham transcript was purportedly pieced together from previous statements Robeson had made, but the fabrication was not uncovered until later. The AP's reporting created an immediate uproar in the US press, with Paul Robeson cast as a "Communist traitor." The frenzy in the press led to many US concert cancellations. The State Department urged the NAACP—which had awarded Robeson its prestigious Spingarn Medal in 1945—to make a statement disassociating themselves from him. When it did, the NAACP denounced him as "tragic," "lost," and even "the Kremlin's stooge."[3] African American baseball star Jackie Robinson was summoned to Washington to appear before the House Un-American Activities Committee to comment on Robeson's speech in a hearing scheduled for July.

Robinson had served as a second lieutenant in the US military, where he had been court-martialed for insubordination after refusing a white driver's orders to move to the back of the bus. As the player responsible for integrating the minor and major leagues, he had faced constant discrimination on and off the field. When racist mutiny struck after he was signed to the Brooklyn Dodgers, with some players deciding they would not share a locker room or even play on the same field as a Black player, they had to be put in line by team manager Leo Durocher, who said, "I do not care if the guy is yellow or black, or if he has stripes like a fuckin' zebra. I'm the manager of this team, and I say he plays. What's more, I say he can make us all rich. And if any of you cannot use the money, I will see that you are all traded."[4]

Robinson was not naïve about what he was being asked to do. Paul Robeson's stature as an actor, singer, and fearless advocate for civil rights had marked him as a man of great talent, integrity, and courage. Robinson looked up to him. He was wary of showing up and later wrote in his autobiography that he could "not help but sense the irony of the fact that I, a Negro once court-martialed for opposing Army Jim Crow, should now be asked to pledge the Negro's loyalty to the Army."[5] Nonetheless, he was convinced to appear by the Dodgers' president and co-owner, Branch Rickey, who had signed him. Rickey was an executive in the Fellowship of Christian Athletes, whose intent was to make the MLB an organization of athletes mobilized to instill Christian values in America's youth. A devoted Methodist, Rickey had once complained that a bishop had "socialistic tendencies" and believed that liberal theology and intellectualism could undermine America's spiritual foundation and lead to Communism.[6] Rickey told Robinson that their "great experiment" of integrating "America's favorite pastime" was on the line and that his testifying "would be the final stroke necessary to establish forever the Negro's place in baseball—and possibly America."[7]

> When he received the invitation to testify before the HUAC, he not only led the National League in batting average, he had also received more votes for the All-Star Game than any other player—proof of his popularity among black and

> white fans alike. A military veteran and devoted Christian who opposed communism, Robinson was viewed as a "Noble Negro," an exemplar of accomplishment and appropriate behavior for black people. That's why the committee chairman turned to him to reassure the nation that black citizens loved America and would defend it against the Soviets.[8]

Robeson returned from Europe just before Robinson's scheduled appearance at the HUAC hearing and attended a rally held in his honor at Rockland Palace in Harlem, where he told the crowd, "We do not want to die in vain anymore on foreign battlefields for Wall Street and the greedy supporters of domestic fascism. If we must die, let it be in Mississippi or Georgia. If we must die, let it be where we are lynched."[9] Robeson, who had been a football All-American in college, an NFL player, and a major supporter of integrating baseball before Robinson was hired by the Dodgers, wrote him a letter insisting that he had been misquoted by the press. When asked about Robeson's Paris speech during the hearing, Robinson responded,

> I've been asked to express my views on Paul Robeson's statement in Paris to the effect that American Negroes would refuse to fight in any war against Russia, because we love Russia so

> much. I haven't any comment on that statement except that if Robeson actually made it, it sounds very silly to me. But he has a right to his personal views and if he wants to sound silly when expressing them in public that's his business and not mine. He is still an ex-athlete and a great singer and actor.[10]

Later in his testimony, Robinson added:

> And one other thing the American public ought to understand, if we are to make progress in this matter: The fact that it is a Communist who denounces injustice in the courts, police brutality, and lynching when it happens doesn't change the truth of his charges. Just because Communists kick up a big fuss over racial discrimination when it suits their purposes, a lot of people try to pretend that the whole issue is a creation of Communist imagination. But they are not fooling anyone with this kind of pretense, and talk about "Communists stirring up Negroes to protest" only makes present misunderstanding worse than ever. Negroes were stirred up long before there was a Communist Party, and they'll stay stirred up long after the party has disappeared—unless Jim Crow has disappeared by then as well.[11]

The next day, Robinson was on the front page of every major US paper with headlines like "Jackie Hits a Double—Against Communists and Jim Crow." Over the course of the next month, before the scheduled concert in Peekskill, Robeson's name was struck from the All-America college football team, and the backlash waved, constant as a flag, across the nation. Newsreel footage of Robeson was destroyed, recordings were erased, concerts and a planned appearance on former First Lady Eleanor Roosevelt's television show were canceled. This laid the backdrop for the growing fury fermenting among anticommunists, racists, and Klansmen in upstate New York, furious that this Communist-loving nigger would dare show his face in their neck of woods. Before Robeson even arrived on the grounds, a mob of locals showed up with baseball bats and rocks, chanting, "dirty Commies," "dirty kikes,"[12] and beating the shit out of concertgoers. Police refused to intervene. Thirteen people were hospitalized in critical condition. An effigy of Robeson was lynched. A giant cross was burned on a hill. One of the best-kept secrets about upstate New York is that it's the Deep South.

The Peekskill concert was canceled and rescheduled to take place a week later by a coalition of unions: the Longshoremen, Fur and Leather Workers, and the United Electric Workers agreed to form a line of defense around the concert grounds. On the day of the concert, twenty thousand people showed up. There was no reported violence over the course of the show, which featured an opening performance by none other than our sporadic church guest and neighbor Pete Seeger!* However, the local racists and political dissenters had not abandoned their aggressive tactics; they had simply decided that this time they would "take the show on the road." As buses of concertgoers left the grounds after the concert, they were detoured from the main highway onto a back road where hundreds of families of local chapters of the Veterans of Foreign Wars and the American Legion were waiting on either side with stones and bricks. They chanted, "Go back to Russia, you niggers," and "white niggers," while smashing bus windows and car windshields.[13] Over 150 people were injured, along with serious damage done to several cars and buses.

After successfully demonizing Robeson in the eyes of the US public, the State Department, upset that he would not stop speaking out—he had since begun to publicly criticize the role of the US in the Korean War, accusing it of using the UN for imperial means—voided Robeson's passport and instructed customs officials to prevent any attempt by him to leave the country.

---

* Pete would eventually be called in front of HUAC as well to discuss his political beliefs. He was sentenced to a year in prison for contempt and blacklisted from appearing on US television until the late 1960s.

So, that is what it meant to be blacklisted. What I was piecing together was that my declaration of wanting to become an actor, an artist, was in some way linked to how an artist might feel a responsibility to use their art to push against injustice and the vindictive measures of any cruel authority, enacted by the highest rungs against the dispossessed, the poor, the oppressed. Wasn't that what Shakespeare was up to with the disarming speech given by Marc Antony in *Julius Caesar*? But now, it was not only the fun and excitement of the stage and its process; I was also being asked to consider the potential danger involved—that acting and entertainment were not necessarily to facilitate a mindless escape or even provide sound commentary but were sometimes in open and direct confrontation. And that an artist might choose to align their work, their choices, with their vision of how the world should be, fully cognizant that the creative vehicle itself might be a means of propaganda enforcing another, less generous vision. That acting was not simply about making choices for a character but that those choices could (and should) be measured against what the specific times demanded of an individual character in service and relation to community and humanity. Actors were not merely functionaries of the stage. The stage was a platform on which the human experience and the relationship between power, ambition, the trivialities of lives in love, worry, and wonder, were all heightened.

But to what purpose? Yes, humor; yes, empathy; yes, insight. Yet, the shortsighted or unquestioned beliefs of a director or writer could serve to enforce unjust power dynamics—and, in some cases, works of art might even be used to heighten them. With modern-day entertainment so deeply coded by commercial success, sequels, and box-office records, it's deeply revealing to consider the United States' first blockbuster: *Birth of a Nation.*

Chapter Four
Violently Antifascist

Birth of a Nation premiered in 1915, the same year that the US invaded Haiti and the first Black world heavyweight boxing champion, Jack Johnson, was defeated. Based on Thomas Dixon's novel *The Clansman: A Historical Romance of the Ku Klux Klan*, *Birth of a Nation* is a mythologized origin story of the Ku Klux Klan as superheroes, set in an deceitful reimagining of the US Civil War and the period of Reconstruction, in which "the former enemies of the North and South are united again in common defense of their Aryan birthright."* The film grossed over $60 million (*not* converted to present-day dollars) at the box office by 1917[1] and was the first film to be shown at the White House.† In accordance with the film's success, Ku Klux Klan hats and aprons were sold as merch at theaters. Ushers dressed in white Klan robes for openings. There were

* The title card from D. W. Griffith's *Birth of a Nation* (1915).

† Thomas Dixon, author of *The Clansman*, was President Woodrow Wilson's classmate at Johns Hopkins University.

Klan-themed balls, and thousands of college students dressed in robes for massive Klan-themed Halloween parties. But the main event was that the Klan itself, defunct since the early 1870s, was revived in Stone Mountain, Georgia, this time with white hoods and burning crosses—both inventions of the film. Lynchings across the US increased fivefold within the first month of its release in January 1915,[2] as white men cosplayed until they became card-carrying members of local chapters. Over the next ten years, the second Klan enrolled millions.[3]

White vigilante mob violence—essential to US settler-colonial origins and expanded beyond the state-sanctioned massacres of the Indigenous population into "nativist" attacks on European immigrants—had, since Emancipation, erupted into massacres of Black Americans across the US landscape. Following the release of *Birth of a Nation*, massacres of Black Americans multiplied into the "Red Summer" of 1919* and continued into the next decades, with no federal interference.

* The outbreak of white-on-Black violence in the summer of 1919 became known as "Red Summer." Riots and deadly attacks occurred in more than two dozen US cities, including Washington, DC, and Chicago; in Elaine, Arkansas, at least two hundred Black citizens were massacred. "Red Summer: The Race Riots of 1919," The National World War I Museum and Memorial, https://www.theworldwar.org/learn/about-wwi/red-summer.

Robeson had founded the American Crusade Against Lynching organization in 1946. W. E. B. Du Bois, Albert Einstein, Lena Horne, and Oscar Hammerstein, along with hundreds of working-class people, were members. Robeson met with President Harry Truman and told him, "If the government doesn't do something about lynching, the Negroes will."[4] He proposed legislation and a plan for educational programs to teach American youth about the treacheries of mob violence. He asked Truman to make a public statement condemning lynching. Truman told him, "Political matters make it difficult to make a statement at this time." In a press conference after their meeting, reporters asked Robeson if he was a Communist. Robeson replied, "I label myself as very violently antifascist," adding that it "seemed inept for the United States to take the lead in the Nuremberg Trials and fall so far behind in respect to justice for Negroes in this country."* The FBI had already classified members of Robeson's organization, such as Einstein, as "Communist sympathizers." They would now classify the American Crusade Against Lynching organization as a "Communist front."

---

* *Pittsburgh Gazette*, September 24, 1946. On the front page where this article was found is another article titled, "Zionists Urge US Pressure: Would Press Truman on Palestine Entry."

It was with this same energy that Robeson filed a suit against the United States to retain his passport. In April 1950, the US District Court for the District of Columbia ruled against the suit, asserting it had no power to act in his case. The State Department filed a brief opposing the suit, "in view of the appellant's frank admission that he has been for years extremely active politically on behalf of the colonial people of Africa."[5] The Justice Department filed another brief, adding, "During his concert tours abroad he has repeatedly criticized the conditions of Negroes in the United States."[6]

That same year, Robeson and Du Bois founded a monthly newspaper, *Freedom*, with the motto, "Where one is enslaved, all are in chains!" *Freedom* gave extensive coverage to trade unions and encouraged its primarily African American readership to identify its struggles with anticolonial movements in Africa, Asia, and the Caribbean, with a strong focus on the struggle against apartheid in South Africa. Three months after the newspaper's first issue, Du Bois was indicted by the US Justice Department as an "unregistered agent of a foreign power" for circulating a petition protesting nuclear weapons, alleging that the petition was Communist propaganda meant to encourage American pacifism in the face of Soviet aggression.[7] A federal judge acquitted Du Bois, as the prosecution failed to present any evidence. However, the State Department successfully confiscated his passport, as it had Robeson's, forbidding him from traveling abroad.

In May 1951, Robeson published an article in *Freedom,* "Conversations about the New China," in which he stated, "I'm for a peace right now that will call all foreign troops out of Korea, certainly including our own boys who are not helping to tear down one single 'colored only' sign by dying in Korea. . . . If we're going to get anywhere against Jim Crow in our own country, we can't do it by letting the man impose Jim Crow on other peoples."[8]

Meanwhile, Robeson was working with the CRC and, along with attorney and activist William Patterson, led its delegation to the United Nations, in December 1951, to formally present the petition "We Charge Genocide: The Crime of the United States Government against the Negro People." Coauthored by Patterson and the CRC and signed by ninety-four US intellectuals and activists, the petition accused the US government of genocide against its Black citizens on the grounds that "some fifteen million black Americans are mostly subjected to conditions making for premature death, poverty, and disease."* The US

---

* This brings to mind prison abolitionist and scholar Dr. Ruth Wilson Gilmore's definition of racism as "the state-sanctioned or extralegal production and exploitation of group-differentiated vulnerability to premature death." Ruth Wilson Gilmore, *Golden Gulag: Prison, Surplus, Crisis,*

government used its influence to have the petition circumvented by preventing the UN Human Rights Commission from discussing the genocide charge.* When Patterson returned to the US, his passport was seized by the State Department so he could no longer speak to foreign audiences about the denial of human rights endured by African Americans and other people of color.[9]

What I was now being prodded to contemplate was that art and artists were as powerful in their influence as information and misinformation from the press, history books, or the nation's highest office. Why else would the State Department involve itself in prohibiting the "free speech" of an artist or cultural figure? In the famous speech that Marc Antony is allowed to give over Caesar's mutilated corpse—under the pretense that he publicly acknowledge that he was speaking only with the permission of the ruling authorities and would say nothing against them—he carefully treads a path to stir mutiny in the hearts of a betrayed people. The play within the play is in pushing through the

---

and Opposition to Globalizing (University of California Press, 2007).

* Sound familiar? See Susan A. Glenn, "We Charge Genocide—The 1951 Black Lives Matter Campaign," Mapping American Social Movements Project, University of Washington, https://depts.washington.edu/moves/CRC_genocide.shtml.

trickery of manipulation used to control the fallout once citizens understand that they have been coerced into thinking that murder is justice, or justified, in exchange for the promise of *freedom* by a handful of men longing for power. Brutus, after participating in the murder of Caesar, attempts to gaslight the Roman citizens, saying:

> If there be any in this assembly, any dear friend of Caesar's, to him I say, that Brutus's love to Caesar was no less than his. If then, that friend demand why Brutus rose against Caesar, this is my answer, Not that I loved Caesar less, but that I loved Rome more. Had you rather Caesar were living and you were slaves, than that Caesar were dead, to live all free men?

An appeal to the love of country was enough to evoke in men, in particular, the muted mind of uniform, to put faith in a higher power and follow orders. In the post–Civil War US, the boastful patriotism of men who enjoyed the spoils of their exploits had a parallel in the poor people who were led to believe the state was shielding them from exploitation while protecting their wives and daughters from the savage "other" at home. This was the *patriarchitecture* of control: a system exacted through racial capitalism that depended not only on the labor of the workers but also on their belief in superiority over "othered" men, women, and workers. That was the science they dropped when, after Emancipation, poor Southern whites, angry at the destitution they now shared with newly freed Black people, began forming militias and threatening insurrection. The government did not respond by giving them money; rather, it gave them "Whites Only" Jim Crow laws to feed their feelings of entitlement and offer the consolation that they might not be rich but would always be considered "better than."

"Jim Crow," the common name given to the South's segregation laws, was derived from the celebrated performances of Thomas D. Rice, known as "The Father of Blackface." Spreading the gospel of anti-Black caricatures and stereotypes was big business long before *Birth of a Nation.* Rice was inspired by a Black disabled stable groom who sang and danced as he worked. Rice is said to have purchased the clothes off the groom's back for "authenticity."[10] Rice's Jim Crow character became the signature act of his traveling show in the early 1830s, often playing to sold-out audiences across the US and Europe. Rice became a rich man, bedecked in "a blue dress coat with gold guineas for buttons, and a vest on which each gold button bore a solitaire diamond."[11] By the late 1830s, "Jim Crow" was a popular pejorative used by white Americans to refer to African Americans.

Here, too, was the influence of art, not just in popularizing phrases, words, and expressions, but in making inextricable connections to the ideologies and conditions they were derived from. Here, art/performance was, essentially, serving as propaganda that not only enforced the status quo but normalized and perpetuated a dynamic of derision and mockery. Of course, this was intentional on Rice's part, although he would have no way of knowing how long that shadow of his work would haunt the American lexicon. Yet, as Robeson pointed out in his denunciation of the 1942 film *Tales of Manhattan*, in which he had a major role, if an artist is not vigilant they may find themselves at the service of the perpetuation of societal wrongs. This is not to say that artists are not capable of writing love songs or creating work that transcends their times, but, without vigorous self-scrutiny, an artist could inadvertently find themselves feeding the machine of their own oppression and that of others. Should one aspire to make *neutral* art? Does Nat King Cole's "Mona Lisa"—or the Mona Lisa itself—fit the bill?

As art historian Jeanne S. M. Willette observed:

> A seemingly neutral Dutch still life from the seventeenth century is also a portrait of the economic dominance of the Dutch in international trade. Men painting women in the nude is an

> expression of male social and economic domination of women and the subordination of women, revealed in paintings which express male desire. The viewer who looks at such paintings as "art," [is] . . . missing the content embedded in the image and [is] inhaling ideology: exploitation of cultures of color and traffic in slavery in the name of capitalism is acceptable; male suppression of women's political aspirations is "normal." Social relations are presumed to be "natural," and, hence, people do not recognize or even realize that the ways they interact are "cultural." Ideology in art remains unseen, and yet it parades itself before the unseeing eyes of the spectator. A work of visual culture expresses the prevailing ideology, not just in terms of what a work of art expresses but also what the work of art does not say.[12]

I suppose, even at my young age, I subconsciously began to see the artist as either an agent of social change or as a producer of work that legitimizes the ruling class. Robeson acknowledged this in his critique of his own early films, realizing that the final product often served to enforce stereotypes he would rather fight to see dismantled, laying the groundwork for his vision of an independent cinema. In a speech he delivered at London's Royal Albert Hall in 1937, during the Spanish Civil War, Robeson proclaimed:

> Every artist, every scientist, must decide NOW where he stands. He has no alternative. There is no standing above the conflict on Olympian heights. There are no impartial observers. Through the destruction—in certain countries—of the greatest of man's literary heritages, through the propagation of false ideas of racial and national superiority, the artist, the scientist, the writer is challenged. The battlefront is everywhere. There is no sheltered rear. . . . What matters a man's vocation or profession? Fascism is no respecter of persons. It makes no distinction between combatants and noncombatants.
>
> The artist must take sides. He must elect to fight for freedom or slavery. I have made my choice. I had no alternative. The history of the capitalist era is characterized by the degradation of my people: despoiled of their lands, their culture destroyed, they are in every country, save one,* denied equal protection of the law, and

* Robeson was referring to his growing admiration for the socialist experiment occurring in the Soviet Union and a principled position on socialism as means of wresting power from the hands of the capitalist class and upending racial domination. He was first invited, in 1934, by Russian

deprived of their rightful place in the respect of their fellows.[13]

Robeson's call to action was in line with what we learned at the workshops we attended during Black History Month, when the kids from the Newburgh Black community would gather to study a fraction of what was simultaneously being broached in newly formed Black and African Studies departments in universities across the country. The workshops were organized by local chapters of Black organizations and churches and had much in common with the Freedom Schools founded by the Student Nonviolent

---

director Sergei Eisenstein, to play the Haitian revolutionary Toussaint L'Ouverture in a film that would never actually get made. Eisenstein also helped arrange a reception and concert in Moscow, where Robeson sang traditional Negro spirituals and four songs he had prepared in Russian. This marked the beginning of what became a mutual love story between Robeson and the Soviet people, who would eventually pack stadiums to hear him sing. Robeson stated that his first visit was the first time he ever felt like a human. The Soviet constitution was praised for its Article 123, which established equality of rights for all citizens, "irrespective of their nationality or race, in all spheres of economic, state, cultural, social, and political life." Advocacy of racial or national exclusiveness, or hatred or contempt, or restrictions of rights and privileges on account of nationality, were to be punished by law. This was, in fact, what African Americans like Robeson were fighting to have added to the US Constitution.

Coordinating Committee, or SNCC, in Mississippi and Alabama in 1964, under the leadership of Kwame Ture (Stokely Carmichael) and a host of students, teachers, and activists. My mother, who was sincerely passionate about teaching, helped organize these programs with other teachers and activists in our community. We studied African art, social and political movements, and different points in our struggle for liberation and equal rights; read poems; memorized names of African nations; had guest speakers; watched plays; and more. I always remember what we learned of the Black Arts Movement of the mid-sixties to seventies that had produced a new generation of artists considered the cultural front of the Black Power movement. These were the contemporaries of our parents, artists who were spoken of as the natural progression of the revered figures from the Harlem Renaissance. There was a certain pride with which they were talked about, as if to say, "Our generation is working on this, too."

I only realize this now. At the time, I simply grasped that the poetry of Jayne Cortez or Sonia Sanchez had the same rich cultural currency as the writings of Claude McKay or Langston Hughes. We learned that artists like Larry Neal and Amiri Baraka, who had founded the Black Arts Repertory Theatre/School in Harlem after the murder of Malcolm X in 1965, had decided that their art should serve a purpose, have a function. And it should function to liberate Black minds. This in itself was no different from what Du Bois had said in "Criteria of Negro Art," a speech he delivered at a 1926 ceremony honoring the historian Carter G. Woodson, who had, that year, pioneered "Negro History Week":

> All art is propaganda and ever must be, despite the wailing of the purists. I stand in utter shamelessness and say that whatever art I have for writing has been used always for propaganda for gaining the right of black folk to love and enjoy. I do not care a damn for any art that is not used for propaganda. But I do care when propaganda is confined to one side while the other is stripped and silent.[14]

But for a new generation, what Kwame Ture helped unleash by placing two words together—one associated with everything evil, unwanted, and ugly, and another that symbolizes the wherewithal to uproot all that displeases and control the means of one's existence—shifted the cultural conversation in ways that sparked the political imagination of colonized people, globally. Black Power became the anthem of the oppressed. It recognized that white people had found a way of codifying their supposed superiority through their frameworks of law and business and that the liberation of the oppressed would be only achieved by taking the matter into our own hands. Black Power sparked the minds not only of leftist organizers and militants but also artists.

Black artists around the world began writing songs about Black Power and Black Pride. Songs about teenage love and heartbreak were now coupled with songs about struggle, standing for your rights, being proud of dark skin and culture. From hairstyles to paintings, graphics, plays, and films, this era is well documented, as are the government crackdowns, murders, and infiltration of organizations like the Black Panther Party, Black Liberation Army, MOVE, and others. What I remember of one particular lesson, held in my father's church, was the person leading the workshop using a hand-carved wooden African spoon as an example and explaining that although it may be beautiful enough to be hung on a wall as a sculpture, it was intended to be used, and an artist should place the same intention into their work, to be of service, and conscious of the fact that our art, in all of its beauty, could be put to pragmatic use.

I've considered this lesson with every artistic release. With the film *Slam*, my intention was to inspire a generation of poets by thoughtfully dissecting popular culture, injecting untaught histories, and fueling the spirit of resistance through words and imagination. I was thinking of poetry as a superpower, able to bend the bars of a prison. Years later, when writing *The Dead*

Emcee Scrolls, I had recently been in conversation with a poet who worked in a juvenile facility and reported that many of the kids might read only one (if any) book a year. I wrote that book imagining every young Black boy who might come across it and at first glance find its small print intimidating and then suddenly find that it was speaking their language. I wanted it to be the first book that you nod your head to, like when listening to an album. Most importantly, I wanted it to address misogyny in the culture in a way that was playful and full of linguistic twists.

The point above about beauty and pragmatism eventually was deepened by my oldest sister, who happened to be away as an exchange student the year I was in third grade. Several years later, she came home from her first semester at Fisk University insisting that we no longer purchase products by a list of companies doing business in or with South Africa—an economic boycott to precipitate an end to apartheid. I decided then, in junior high school, to dedicate a social studies report, due after the holiday break, to South African apartheid. At that time, there were an estimated eight thousand students being held in South African detention centers—prisons—for protesting the Bantu Education forced on them in the inhumane system of racial segregation and discrimination that required Black South Africans to carry passbooks—internal passports—to report to work or leave the townships they were forced to live in. There had been massacres and there were political prisoners, along with a host of exiled artists, like Miriam Makeba and Hugh Masakela. Our passion in wanting to see an end to South African apartheid relied on the fact that, unlike the stories and images we knew of the civil rights movement, this was happening now. Those student leaders and protesters disappeared, and often murdered, in South African prisons were our age and students like us! This was not Black History, this was the present, which made it all the more urgent, especially considering that this was happening on African soil, in the homeland of those who were being oppressed.*

* This was the moment I first learned about Israel as a collaborator with the apartheid regime. South African diamonds were mined and transported to Israel to avoid economic sanctions and boycotts before hitting the market as "Israeli diamonds," in exchange for Israeli weapons and military vehicles used by white South African police. The fact that the US government and corporations played a hand in facilitating this was the point I would use, in my school report, to drive my point home. My sister gave me a quote from Henry David Thoreau's essay "Civil Disobedience": "What I have to do is to see, at any rate, that I do not lend myself to the wrong which I condemn." And that quote, which, from then on, operated like a personal mantra, offered a finishing coat for how I would not only internalize but actualize the primer of individual responsibility inspired by that first Robeson report. It made sense of the agency I had to operate in my personal and creative life. I could not contribute to any wrong that I

Engaging in a boycott against South African apartheid was significant for me because it solidified an internationalist relationship to dispossessed, poor, and Black people outside of the United States. My actions in New York could target and impact the lives of those under oppressive or colonial rule in other places. We stopped purchasing Coca-Cola products, no longer bought gas from Shell, and boycotted other companies doing business in South Africa. Being immune to the patriotic fervor built into the American machine didn't limit my awareness of the military and financial power that the nation exerted outside of its borders. This, too, was woven into the fabric of cultural self-aggrandizement peddled to American citizens. "The most powerful nation in the world." "A nuclear power." "A superpower." "Leader of the free world." And then there was the massive cultural influence: the films, music, and pop stars promulgated throughout the world. Aside from knowing that Michael Jackson was a global phenomenon, I hadn't really considered looking at Hollywood's highly financed blockbusters as the stories the US chose to tell about itself, or at the underlying messages in these stories—how they might serve to foster patriotism or exceptionalism in the

---

had already determined as wrong. This did not narrow the world for me; it opened it. It sharpened my sense of humor and strengthened my ability to say, "Fuck that."

American psyche and serve as propaganda for viewers in other nations.

I would learn firsthand of this influence a few years later, when I decided to follow that spark my sister lit for me in the third grade and become an exchange student. In the summer of 1988, at the age of sixteen, I traveled to Brazil for my junior year of high school.* The time in Brazil deepened what would become a more global understanding of music, class, and race.

---

* It's important to point out that these were not dreams our parents could necessarily afford; rather, they had made it clear that there would always be a way to facilitate achieving our goals even if they didn't have the money to support them. My dad, of course, would say, "The Lord will make a way out of no way." We researched scholarships, participated in academic contests with financial awards, and, of course, pooled resources from the community. That was how my sister discovered that an organization called the Rotary Club sponsored students on foreign exchange. Otherwise, there was a constant stream of special offerings at church to help students pay their tuition, or a church member buy a ticket to attend a family member's funeral, or the like. This understanding that we didn't need to be rich to experience the world was the privilege that we exercised.

Chapter Five

Race and Class Revelation to the Beat of the Drum

My experience in Brazil was permeated by tender instruction. I wandered streets and neighborhoods, took long bus rides, frequented nightclubs, bars, and cafés, talking to strangers. The dichotomy between how my Blackness was perceived versus my Americanness, which is to say my response to the question of where I was from, played out openly before me as I witnessed twisting perceptions at work. American pop culture had enchanted the Brazilian youth and convinced them of America's *freeness* and power. Having to perpetually explain that I was not rich, that the American system was corrupted by racism, that police were the enemy there, too—"cop-aganda," like the show *C.H.I.P.S.*, had been syndicated, adding a veneer of cool as a cover-up—helped shape my understanding of how American entertainment was a major tool used to propagandize the state.

In Goioerê, a small town in the middle of an agricultural paradise, in the southern state of Paraná, my host family told me that the public high school I was expected to attend was only in session at night because anyone over fifteen was expected to be working in the fields during the day. As a sixteen-year-old African American New Yorker, working in the fields sounded nothing like paradise to me, but luckily my first host family was not in the agricultural business, so farm work was not in my cards. Neither was school, it turned out. For the first four months of the school year, teachers across Brazil were on strike for better salaries, improved work conditions, and more educational autonomy.* To make up for the fact there was no school, my host mother took the time to give me Portuguese lessons every morning, followed by my translating the lyrics of some of the music I had brought with me, like Public Enemy and Sade, into Portuguese.

My host mother was a stay-at-home mom. The two eldest sons had moved to the big city—Londrina and São Paolo, respectively—and the youngest, who was twelve, became my local tour guide until I learned the streets and began to wander by myself. The family had a maid, who came every day except Sunday. She was

* The strike was led by Central Única dos Trabalhadores (Central Unified Workers), a national trade union that had been instrumental in pressuring for the redemocratization of Brazil while it was under US military rule from 1964 to 1985.

the first Black person I met in Brazil. It was also my first time living with a family with a maid. The family didn't strike me as rich, yet they clearly lived comfortably and were upwardly mobile, as was evidenced by their membership in the local Rotary Club. My parents were not in the Rotary Club. When I attended a local meeting before my departure for Brazil, I knew none of the families there. In Newburgh, Rotary was completely white. Yet, the members didn't seem to be particularly rich. In Brazil, or in Goioerê at least, belonging to the Rotary Club seemed to confer a higher social status. I attended the monthly meetings with my host family and met most of the well-to-do members of the community. They owned big farms, businesses, architectural firms, hotels, and the like. All of the families were either white passing or Asian.

One of the other two exchange students in town introduced me to the local popular *barzinho*, where local teens and young adults hung out. As a young hip-hop head, fresh out of New York, the first thing that stood out to me was that most of the guys were wearing high-waisted jeans and cowboy boots. Inside the small café-like bar, an acoustic guitar player accompanied by a person on percussion sang what I later learned were songs from David Bowie's *The Rise and Fall of Ziggy Stardust and the Spiders from Mars* in Portuguese.*

* This was my first encounter with songs like "Five Years," "Starman," and "Moonage Daydream." It would take a few

The percussion was a nice touch, with distinct Brazilian rhythms. I was into it. With time, I'd spend long hours listening to musicians play inside the bar, but on that first night and for quite some time after, it was as if I was an astronaut returning from space. The kids would gather around and ask me questions about the US. Was it really like in the movies? Was I fan of Michael Jackson? Were the college campuses as wild as they were in popular films? Were the high schools really like that—with lockers, football teams, cheerleaders, and bloody proms? Was America really free? One question initially caught me off guard, but I was asked it so often that I eventually got used to it: "What was it like to get sprayed with a fire hose?"*

---

more years before I discovered that these were not merely popular Brazilian songs, written in Portuguese.

* Months later, when (night) school did eventually begin, teachers placed me in the middle of the classroom so that they and students could ask me questions about films, TV shows, superheroes, popular musicians, civil rights, and "freedom." Before I left the US, it had been determined by my high school in Newburgh that none of my grades in Brazil would count toward my US academic record, as it was assumed that Brazil's educational system was inferior to ours. Thus, since I was now fluent in Portuguese, and because my presence at school proved so disruptive, my host family decided that I didn't necessarily need to go. Yet, I went at first because I was so happy to see faces of color and kids who seemed to belong to the same social class as me. I made a few friends, developed a few crushes, but

I spent my days at the country club my host family was a member of, playing pool, ping pong, or tennis, which my host brother had taught me how to play, doing deep dives into French and Asian cinema with rented cassettes, or, my favorite pastime, wandering the streets. Consistently, I'd walk into a small shop or cafe and hear a swift "sssyuu" and see someone behind a counter shooing me away with their hand, as if I were a straggler looking for a handout. I'd typically respond, in English, "Excuse me?," they'd ask where I was from, and then they'd offer me a chair so they could ask me what it was like to be sprayed with a firehose, lol. At the time, what I perceived was that, to them, in the southern farmland of Brazil, being Black meant that I was poor—yet, being American meant that I was rich. Mind you, Brazil has a larger population of formerly enslaved Africans than any other country in the diaspora, including the US, but in my small city this was hardly apparent.

There were two major high points of my time with my second family.* The first was the house itself. The second was our short, weeklong trip to Rio de Janeiro. This host family was Japanese. I learned then that the

---

mostly hung out in the classroom with the English teacher I had befriended during the strike, as she was also my host brother's capoeira instructor.

* It was planned by the Rotary Club that I would live with three different families (four months with each).

largest population of Japanese people outside of Japan is in Brazil. Japanese people began migrating to Brazil in the early 1900s and were responsible for a great deal of the coffee and soybean cultivation. My host family owned a large sugarcane plantation in the north of the country. Their sugarcane was processed into ethanol, which many cars across the country, including theirs, ran on. Mark this, 1989, as my first time learning of alternative fuels in a material fashion.

In addition to being a businessman, the dad was a Buddhist priest. There was a temple with a towering golden Buddha built into the house. An architectural dream, with a large open-air garden in its center, encased by glass walls, the house had been built to surround a greenhouse. "My room" was a double-doored, soundproof, wooden listening room that had a stereo built into its walls, including two huge wooden speakers, two cassette decks, a CD player, radio, and record player, its own bathroom, and a single bed. I was told I could play music at any volume, and it would not disturb the rest of the house. There was an intercom system built into every room, so the songs of two birds who lived in the back of the house were a constant companion. Again, my host family had a Black maid. Now that I was mostly fluent in Portuguese, there was less of a language barrier. When I asked her where she lived and if I could visit her home, she laughingly responded, "But you're rich, you don't need to see that."

It was admittedly strange to explain to someone, while living in the lap of luxury and basking in the privilege of international travel, not as a migrant but as a visitor, that I was, in fact, not rich. Less strange to express that I wanted to see and connect with other Black people. I had that opportunity, not at her house, but on a visit to Rio.

It wasn't just that I had my ears opened to whole new world of sound, intricate rhythms, and melodic innovations, but the time alone, without school, gave me the chance to dive into music I may or may not have heard, on the level of albums, deep dives, genres, and repeated listens. There's a bootleg of James Brown's *Live at the Apollo,* from 1972, that I know as intricately as my own home. The white girl exchange student from Washington State turned me on to Sinead O'Connor, the Smiths, Morrissey . . . but I loved listening to the radio in Brazil. On the long car ride to Rio de Janeiro, I marveled at the muscular cows, the terraced cultivation of the farms, and the distinction of the rhythms from those that I was used to, on the radio. There was a playful mastery in melodies that paralleled watching the way a capoeira master, when sparring with a child, would leave them spinning, punching and kicking the air, as the master's swift, graceful movements said, "I'm on my head," "I'm over your head," "I'm behind you."

For the duration of my visit, I'd been vibing with Brazilian music: the popular songs on the radio, in live performances at the barzinho, and on television shows. The first song that caught my ear on the radio was called "Madagascar," by a group called Olodum. The breadth of the drumming, in a contemporary song, as part of the daily countdown no less, caught me off guard. Loud African drums played in a rhythm that felt both ceremonial and for marching; I was in it from the jump. I struggled to understand the lyrics, but the refrain was clearly about the large island off the east coast of Africa. Picking out the words I understood from the verses was more difficult. The first two that stuck out were "negras verdades," which, to my immediate understanding, meant "real niggas," but in the context of the song, which is about the precolonial history of the Malagasy people and the Imerina Kingdom—the cross-section of peoples who made up the population—and their struggle against colonization and apartheid, it meant "dark truths." "Madagascar" very easily and quickly became a personal anthem. I purchased the album, blasted it in my room, and traveled with it in my Walkman. It's fascinating to think about what I listened to, discovered, and learned about music while in Brazil.

When I visited Rio with my hosts, Spanish tourists crowded around me, mistaking me for Dwayne Wayne from *A Different World* because of the flip-up spectacles I had purchased for five bucks on the streets of New York before departing. At some point during our sightseeing, I was on the steps beneath the Cristo Redentor statue on the Corcovado Mountain overlooking the favelas—the Black "slums" that surround Rio. I was more impressed by the sight of the favelas than I was by the statue or the view of the sea. In every direction, the hills and mountainsides surrounding this precious city were another form of tiered cultivation.

Class distinctions were jarring—they reminded me of what I had seen the summer before third grade, when I took my first international trip, to Haiti, to visit my grandfather, who was living in Port-au-Prince.* My memories of that first trip to Haiti, aside from bonding with my cousin—who was my age and would later come to live with us, in Newburgh—revolve mostly around the bold, bright, contrasting-patterned clothes people wore, green lush mountains, winding roads, raw sugarcane, and a magical black-sand beach. Yet, on that trip, I also began to develop a grasp on the gradations between wealth disparities in the Global North and the reality on the ground for the global majority. Here it was again, in Rio de Janeiro. I was also beginning to see New York differently. The music was a part of that.

* My grandparents on my mother's side landed at Ellis Island from Haiti in 1919, during the thirty-four-year US occupation. Grandma Charlemagne, as we called my great-grandmother, had emigrated alone at the age of twenty-three. Although she had passed before I entered third grade, I remember her well.

Down the mountainside were exquisite, gated homes and beneath them sprawling ramshackle developments. At the entrance to the city, young kids made a business of standing in parking spots on crowded streets, waving drivers in, and accepting cash to watch your car. These were the same kids, I later learned, targeted by death squads comprised of off-duty and ex-cops, who, according to Rio's National Movement for Street Children, assassinated 4,611 kids between January 1988 and December 1990.[1] I did not know these statistics at the time, yet the class disparity between the families I lived with and the Black and brown populations I was now seeing bore evidence of a system that was clearly not working the same way for everyone. And, although this was also true of the US, the familiarity I may have felt with my hood in Newburgh, or Black neighborhoods I had been exposed to through visiting friends and family in Harlem, Brownsville, East New York, Nashville, Flint, DC, Philly, Baltimore, Richmond, and Galveston—the favelas were a whole other story.

Contrasting with the seductive bossa nova and samba rhythms that flowed from beachside cafés, it was via the street kids in Rio that I finally heard hip-hop in Brazil. I was so excited to hear our local music abroad, to know that our "virus" was spreading. I had brought with me more than a dozen cassettes of the latest hip-hop albums. The one with the heaviest rotation in my sound-proof, boombox bedroom—and also in my headphones, no doubt—was an album that had come out just a week before my departure and was simply my most prized possession: *It Takes a Nation of Millions* by Public Enemy. I had been listening to Public Enemy since their debut single, "Public Enemy Number One," hit New York airwaves in '87. I remember being at my boy's crib after school, with a boombox on the front porch, losing our shit the first time we heard it. There are many other songs, like "Eric B. Is President," Marley Marl's "The Symphony," Ultramagnetic MC's "Funky," Boogie Down Productions' "The Bridge Is Over," or "The Style You Haven't Done Yet," that share the distinction of my remembering where I was, who I was with, the first time I heard them. The energy we felt around early hip-hop in New York was beyond pride.

We felt like emissaries of a new technology that was being born organically.* Positioning the drums up front, fattening the bass, using the speaking voice instead of the singing voicc, conjuring dances with rhythm, owning the language, operated in us like a spiritual possession. And in that spirit of vibrant innovation that encapsulated our African roots and defiant positioning of being born into a fucked-up world that would rather kill or imprison us than see us as human,

* I would encounter this feeling again, traveling as a young poet during the rise of "slam poetry" and "spoken word."

a new generation was voicing an outright refusal to play by any rules but its own. I felt like I owned hip-hop. We all did. It came with its own attitude and re-programmed our listening.

Public Enemy epitomized a point in the journey where the production, the samples of noise, sirens, snippets from speeches, punctuated by many—in particular, chopped-up James Brown—beats and rhythms, in ways that highlighted and formed new beats and rhythms, was *evenly yoked* by a staccato vocal delivery that put politics on the level of the drums, up front. "Rebel Without a Pause," "Black Steel in the Hour of Chaos," "Bring the Noise"—these songs, for the times, it seemed, crystallized hip-hop as an anticolonial art form and platform for a new generation determined to face struggle with confidence, swagger, and pride. I had spent years defending hip-hop to adults and white kids in school who would argue that it wasn't even music . . . until they heard the Beastie Boys. But Public Enemy deaded all that by sharpening the vision. I would argue that most international hip-hop movements in hoods and ghettoes across the world were formed after the inspiration of Public Enemy. They solidified the movement of word sound power as a vehicle of resistance. It was the warrior music of the disenfranchised or, as Chuck D put it, "the Black CNN."

Another album I had traveled with was Boogie Down Productions' *By All Means Necessary.** They had changed the game with their album *Criminal Minded.* It wasn't just that the rapper, KRS-ONE, had dusted MC Shan and the Juice Crew with his battle-rap anthem "The Bridge Is Over," but his cadence and style as a lyricist instantly made all the rap that came before it sound dated. MCs started changing their style up just to keep up with where the music was heading. But KRS-ONE was substance *and* style. He had been a homeless teenager when he met his social worker, Scott Sterling, at a men's shelter in the Bronx. Scott was also a DJ and beat producer. Along with another DJ, D-Nice, they formed Boogie Down Productions and, in 1987, made it clear not only that hip-hop had started on their turf in the South Bronx but also that

* This was an album that completely transformed hip-hop. KRS's dexterity and wit, coupled with a seemingly hard-earned street knowledge and sense of self made it one of the earliest examples of "gangster rap," "conscious rap," and "battle rap," at the same time. It played a major role in redefining hip-hop for what was technically the third generation of rappers (the first wave being Mellie Mel, Spoonie Gee, the Sugarhill Gang, and others; the second wave being Run DMC, Salt & Pepa, and others. KRS and his contemporaries Public Enemy and Rakim were the newest wave of where this very young art form might head, both beat-wise and through spoken cadence and wit. It was all very exciting.

rap was poetry.* Their first album, *Criminal Minded,* took New York by storm. I may have put a full ten thousand hours into that album. This was before we had categories like "underground," "gangster," "backpacker," or "conscious." Although there had certainly been breakthrough groups and hits, in this time period practically all hip-hop was underground.

We listened to two main stations in New York, WBLS and KISS-FM. They played the newly pressed vinyl of the local talent who were speaking the language of our subconscious yearning for bass- and kick-driven soundscapes where human voices shared speech-patterned swagger. It felt as if we were carving a future, with found objects, mixed media, and dances reflecting it. A few nights a week, the respective radio DJs would play their prerecorded voice-drops announcing "World Premiere! World Premiere!" and some beat

---

* Boogie Down Productions' single "Poetry," off their first album, *Criminal Minded,* was quite the talk piece for those of us who had to defend hip-hop to our parents or peers who failed to understand why would get so excited about someone talking or storytelling over a beat. KRS openly identifying as poet served to clarify the art form for outsiders who needed to know how they should approach appreciating the music. Suddenly the assertion "They're just talking" could be defended by "It's poetry!" And for many, that was enough. For me, it just resonated as brilliance. I was projecting my idea of the future into the music. Why wouldn't I, when we spent half the time dancing like robots?

would come through the system, immediately capture your imagination, make you scrunch your face up and nod your head like you were in deep agreement in a conversation that you'd been dying to have, and then some voice would come through, and absolutely nothing would come between you and listening. KRS-ONE would often use a soft Jamaican patois with an unmistakable edge that was razor-sharp and schooled. He called himself "the teacher." He referenced his work as poetry and confessed that he really didn't want to battle. The work was to teach. New styles substanced by thought. The beats were jagged and rudimentary but with just enough swing to let you know that it was what it was. The tragedy was that his partner and DJ, Scott Sterling, aka Scott La Rock, was murdered just five months after the release of *Criminal Minded*. The release following Scott's murder, *By All Means Necessary*, showed that KRS-ONE—whose name stood for Knowledge Reigns Supreme Over Nearly Everyone—was sharp, combative, and focused, through the loss of his mentor, to become the mentor to his listeners:

> "A vegetarian/no goat or ham/or chicken, or turkey, or hamburger/'cause to me that's suicide/self-murder . . ."[2]

> "I do not contemplate a battle, 'cause it really ain't worth it/I'd rather point a pistol at your head and try to burst it!/I'm teaching poetry!"[3]

Lol. I was so fucking hooked.

I began rapping in the third grade, too. My first raps were playful attempts to write rhymes in Old English or using words and phrases I learned in French class. Upon hearing T La Rock's "It's Yours," I began developing a style that challenged me to broaden my vocabulary and pace my flow in a way that was yielding results in lunch-table battles and cyphers. When I started, I would steal legal pads from my father's office, put a star at the end of every other line—where it needed to rhyme—and fill in the blanks. By the time I got to Brazil, I had reams of raps, mostly memorized, and had already battled every rapper in my city and any other city, church, or school I'd visited. The fact that I was fully identified as a rapper in a small town like Goioerê, where I, at first, had to explain what hip-hop was, should have, perhaps, been more off-putting, yet I was learning so much about other music that I was actually good.

Music was a bonding point with many of the Brazilians I met. Even my first host father, whom I found to be overly "macho" and maybe not so pleased that a Black exchange student had arrived to live with his family, turned me on to some great fucking music.

And once he saw that I was enjoying it, turned me on to some more. The album he played most often, which I was certain to leave with a copy of, was *Os Mutreteiros Grilados.* Later, I learned that it was a rather unknown band comprising studio musicians who had played with the greats—much like the Funk Brothers, the Motown backing band that played on dozens of hit records with celebrity lead singers, yet little was known about the musicians backing them.

One of the best friends I made at the local barzinho was in his mid-twenties and had served as an apprentice for a man who molded and made dentures. He was funny as fuck. With no school to go to, some afternoons I would wander to his wooden storefront laboratory and chill with him as he made false teeth and played me popular Brazilian music. That was the first time I ever really listened to punk. There was a song he would blast and we would lose our shit to, "Policia," by a popular group called Titãs. The way they belted the chorus—"Policia para quem precisa! Policia para quem precisa de policia!"—had a level of "fuck the police" energy that I felt in my chest. I was in a constant state of discovery, in terms of music, food, culture, yet because I found most of it agreeable, I was rarely uncomfortable.

We returned to Goioerê during Carnival season. Absolutely nothing could have prepared me. My sister had not mentioned Carnival in any memorable way.

Six days of continuous drumming, owing its sonic evolution to the enslaved West Africans comprising the largest African population outside of Africa. I had never stood surrounded by hundreds of drums on all sides so that the sound poured into me and caught me unaware.

Local friends and I linked arms and danced in circles around a track field, while drummers and percussionists filled the stands of the stadium, where typically the audience would sit to watch a game. Stop to eat, stop to sleep, it's still going, all day and all through the night. The songs and costumes spoke of the Indigenous and African origins of the country, the Portuguese colonizers, the wretchedness of slavery, the fabric of Brazil—and everybody took part, sang along, danced. I remember thinking, "Nah, we don't have nothing like this," although, at that time I had not yet been to New Orleans or experienced Mardi Gras, but that was restricted to Louisiana or to those who knew and shared that history. I knew the West Indian Day parade in Brooklyn, which was more of a culture clash and celebration of the Caribbean diaspora in New York. Brazilian Carnival was nationwide, for everyone. It felt like a unified celebration of the nation's horrid past, captured in song by its survivors, dancing through their history. I didn't even peep that it was supposed to be a religious celebration starting the Friday before Ash Wednesday, the beginning of

Lent. All I saw were legs moving and constant invitations to dance. I'm not ashamed to say that this was my first time crying on the dance floor.

If drum intoxication is a thing, that's what I felt. My mind was spinning in a million "What ifs?" What if African Americans had held so strongly to our African traditions? What if our traditional drums had not been stripped from us by insidious colonial laws that bore open witness to the fact that, through music, we are not only communicating with each other but with something greater than our individual selves? What if the US decided to dance to our history instead of banning it? What if we never had to defend the grittiness of the blues, the swing of jazz, the headiness of bebop, the cornerstones of soul and funk, the origins of rock and roll, the rawness of hip-hop, and we all just celebrated it as proof of the colonial and genocidal chaos that we survived? What if the Indigenous people had maintained their protectorship of the land and gave us the condition of honoring it? I ain't saying that's what the music said, or what the songs, or Carnival itself, were about. These were the thoughts running through my head as a result of the rhythms, costumes, and songs. There, at sixteen years old, I attempted to imagine the conditions and distinctions in cultural practices among Portuguese, British, Spanish, and French slavers and colonialists.

It had been easy to imagine that the chattel slavery of Africans—a form of slavery distinguished from other existing forms of indentured slavery because the chattel, or "cattle," slave was not considered human—had been the same everywhere throughout the diaspora, but now I was forced to reckon with marked distinctions beyond geography and language. The most obvious example was between the French and the British/American, with the "one drop rule," the US law that stipulated that if you had one drop of African blood you were to be classified as Black. The unwritten law in Haiti and Louisiana under French rule, by contrast, was practically the opposite. If you had one drop of French blood, you were free and considered part of the *gens de couleur libres,* the free people of color, basically a third class of "mixed" people. This distinction was common in Spanish and French colonies. It constitutes the caste system responsible for much of the "colorism" still prevalent in much of the colonized world, including the US, today. In the colonial US, free people of color had rights that were forbidden to enslaved Africans, such as the rights to education, to marry, to own land; however, they did not have the right to vote. "Mixed" women were often sold to white slaveholders as concubines or pushed into prostitution, which birthed another fanged stereotype, the "Jezebel." In *Birth of a Nation,* these were the people characterized as the biggest threat to the sanctity of whiteness. In many cases, this system built a divide between the educated "mixed" class and enslaved Africans, although, in Haiti, it was the solidarity between the gens de couleur, enslaved Africans, and the Indigenous people that ultimately defeated the French.[4]

Unlike in the US, Brazil's Indigenous population was also enslaved during its colonial era, a clear colonial distinction that marked the culture differently. Yet, during the Atlantic slave trade, Brazil imported more enslaved Africans than any other slaveholding colony. African slaves were more expensive than Indigenous slaves, primarily because the average life span of an Indigenous worker was nineteen years, while the average life span of enslaved Africans was twenty-three.[5] There were no segregation laws or bans on interracial marriage in Brazil, thus ethnic mixing was much more prevalent and visible. This was a reality that, because of my own colonial indoctrination, I became fascinated by, at the time. That year, in Brazil, I'd see someone with my dark complexion and gray eyes or arresting combinations of features and beauty strains that sometimes caught me off guard and had me questioning whether there was anything more beautiful.

The eugenic practice common in Brazil is known as *branqueamento*, or "whitening," an ideology that proposed the closer to white an individual or family appeared, the higher in rank they could achieve in society. For this reason, in Brazil, many people "passed" as white, whereas, to the Black American eye, we might be, like, "Um, somebody's got a secret to tell." For those too dark to pass, a census conducted during my time in Brazil found that most Brazilians self-identified as over three hundred different "races." In addition to "mixed," "pardo," "mulatto," and "moreno," Brazilians consistently used terms like "coffee with milk," "cinnamon," "light nut," "dark nut," "burnt white," and others.[6] The bottom line could easily be interpreted as anti-Blackness and a decision to be identified as anything but Black—yet our own social conditioning, perhaps, plays a strong hand in that analysis.

Either way, at the age of sixteen, I was just coming out of an early adolescence in which I, too, had internalized a level of self-hate that was, unfortunately, commonplace. From the ages of thirteen to fifteen, I kept a regular supply of Ambi, a product that on its packaging was said to remove blemishes, yet in its fine print was what is most commonly referred to as a "skin bleaching cream." It was as if my complexion was one huge blemish I was looking to remove. Commentary and jokes about my complexion had, in fact, gotten to me.

In Brazil, I came to appreciate the uniqueness of each individual appearance. Bushy eyebrows, thick lips, varied complexions, hair colors, and features seemed to say, "God don't make ugly. This can only get more and more interesting." A little later on, I began to develop little theories about the types of thoughts and hidden beliefs we harbor and how the ugliness or beauty of these dispositions always seems to push through the eyes and soul of a person, making those who, according to beauty standards, might be characterized as "unattractive" attractive, or vice versa. I tried to monitor my inner world and how it was projected outward.

A few months later, I began to test these theories in accordance with my developing viewpoints on a month-long trip across Brazil, into the northeast and the Amazon, with fifty other exchange students from across the world. I would be meeting a lot of new people, and I wanted to be more engaging, to find things to compliment in people, to find admirable traits and perhaps even nurture them.* The trip—a full-on package tour—was arranged by the Brazilian Rotary association, for students who could afford it. My godfather purchased my ticket as a gift for my seventeenth birthday. Our first stop was Salvador, Bahia.

---

* I have no idea why I decided to engage in this way. Perhaps because I had grown up in a small town where there weren't a lot of new encounters. We all knew each other. This lessened the feasibility of reinvention. This trip would be an opportunity to reinvent myself and see if I could be less withdrawn and observant, more engaged . . .

Now that I've been to New Orleans, I can say that traveling to Salvador was akin to traveling to NOLA. Although Pequena África ("Little Africa") in Rio de Janeiro is credited with being the birthplace of samba, capoeira, and Candomblé—the Brazilian spiritual practice with roots in West African traditions, carefully blended with Catholicism, much like Haitian Vodou or Cuban Santería, centered around *orixas,* or saints, conceived as ancestral figures or embodied forces of nature—Salvador was a cultural landmark. Walking through the old city, I was immersed in community that beckoned back to its African roots in ways that felt familiar: traditional head wraps, West African symbols and art that referenced Brazil's colonial past, and food that bore a resemblance to what we call "down-home" cooking. My time in Salvador provided a kind of backbone to my understanding of the African roots in many aspects of Brazilian culture.

In the heart of the Amazon, I learned about Manaus, the richest city in South America during the heights of the rubber trade of the late 1800s, a time that corresponded directly with the genocide of Indigenous people throughout the region. In places like the Congo and Asia, local populations were corralled into slavery to meet the growing European and white American demands for rubber, used to make tires for the newly developing automobile industry. Despite this harsh reality more than a hundred years removed from my arrival, the Indigenous presence was everywhere in Manaus, as was architecture that spoke to the time when the city was the home to rich colonial barons. Most remarkable were the *palafitas*, wooden houses built on stilts, near the river where many Indigenous families lived. We took a boat to where the calm, black waters of the Rio Negro met the brown rushing waters of the Amazon. As soon as the tip of the boat touched the Amazon we were swept into its roaring waters. We pulled into coves where small Indigenous villages sold fish, slingshots, machetes, baskets, and more. Some kids carried large snakes on their shoulders, charging minimal fees to hold and be photographed with the snakes. One of our guides purchased a small goat, which he brought back on the boat with us. When we reached another small cove, where the water was calm, with no village in sight, we were invited to jump off the boat and swim. After about an hour in the water, we all climbed back on board and the guide picked up the little goat, slit its throat, and threw it in the water. Within seconds, the goat was devoured by piranha. We followed long trails through the forest. The scale of the trees, the scope of greenery, stays with me. Perhaps most impressive were the gigantic, ancient rubber trees, whose folded roots enveloped us in sunken histories.

Back in Manaus, my most memorable night was in a nightclub, when the DJ spun New Order's

"Blue Monday," and a tall, handsome brown man, who seemed to be older than most of us—in a balloon-sleeved, flowing white shirt, tucked into high-waisted pants, as was the Brazilian style at the time—proceeded to lift his arms and, oh so subtly, move his hands in a way that felt like he was orchestrating the dance floor and perhaps the night itself. I document it here because, to this day, this man and his movements have haunted me as the North Star of cool in relation to music, nightlife, and style. Perhaps he was my guardian angel—as I soon embarked on a much sketchier trip, with a Belgian friend I became close to while traveling with this group of exchange students. It was through conversations with the other exchange students, particularly those from Europe and Canada, that I began to piece together distinctions between the US capitalist system and its European counterparts. For instance, I was shocked to learn that none of my young Scandinavian friends, who were all preparing to go to college, had concerns about the price of education. They would all be attending universities, regardless of their field of study, where the tuition was primarily covered by the state. Not because they were outstanding students—simply because of their status as a citizen. I would ask questions like, "But if you decide to become a doctor or lawyer, those schools must be very expensive, right?" No, it was simply a matter of making a choice about your field and fulfilling the proper academic requirements—the tuition was still primarily covered by the state. Likewise, discussions about healthcare were equally informative. Medical debt was simply not a thing in these countries. The unbridled capitalism of the US system was so deeply intertwined with racism that I had no real question as to why it was not the same at home, but it struck me then that providing healthcare and education should be the obligation of a country that boasted of power, riches, freedom, and democracy. This was perhaps my earliest understanding of socialism and of what the Santee Sioux poet John Trudell meant when he said that US politicians speak of freedom to avoid speaking of responsibility.[7]

I finished the group trip, dropped my bags in Goioerê, grabbed a backpack, and caught a bus to meet up with my Belgian friend. We were interested in seeing more cities and more nightclubs, and this time we wanted to travel by bus, to see the gaps we had flown over when traveling with the larger group. Our plan was simple: catch a bus to a distant town or city, find the local nightclub, dance all night, and repeat. And that's pretty much what happened. We'd arrive in a town, find the local hangout; people would ask where we were from (we definitely stood out by the way we dressed,[8] which is probably why we clicked), invite us to hang out, introduce us to their friends, maybe offer a shower, take us to the club; we'd stay 'til about 4 a.m., get a ride to the bus station, choose the next destination, sleep on the bus, arrive in a new town, and do it again. The buses offered a glimpse into the countryside and everyday life, which we were hungry for after a month of plane rides, hotels, and guided tours. The long hours I spent in headphones, studying music, letting thoughts dance with questions, dreaming, reflecting on what I had experienced, been taught, what I hadn't been taught, forming hypotheses, sometimes writing them down, or simply focused on a rhyme pattern, a vocal technique, the contours of a beat or bass line.

That may be the only year of my life that I don't remember reading. In Brazil, I was a listener, an observer. My parents had treated "bored" like a bad word the first time I tried to use it. From then on, I made shadows dance, read dictionaries and encyclopedias, read and reread the *Complete Works of Shakespeare,* freestyled and recited lyrics while walking the streets, made up games, gave myself personal challenges. These habits followed me until the buses I took in Brazil turned into tour buses. Of course, my friend and I were benefiting from male and Western privilege. The fact that we had no serious run-ins, had little fear of being taken advantage of, and could float freely, relying simply on people's well-meaning curiosity is not afforded to everyone. Yet this wandering spirit has stayed with me and has served as a kind of passport that has continually inspired me to talk to strangers.

When my time in Brazil ended, I returned to Newburgh, New York, in a state of quiet reflection. The local newspaper decided to interview me about the trip—a small-town wonder. I attempted to articulate the interest that was aroused in people who had not had many run-ins with American tourists (the only other US citizens I ran into during my year away were young white Mormon evangelicals). I recounted the abrupt dismissal I experienced in local shops as a Black person, until they discovered I was American, and how that somehow made all the difference. I spoke of wealth disparity, how I had not witnessed much of a middle class, only the very rich and the very poor, and that Black people were a majority among the poor. That 80 percent of Black women in Brazil worked as domestic servants. That inflation went up 861 percent while I was there; in fact, Brazil had changed its currency twice during my stay. How my host families would watch the news every day to see the current exchange rate, and that the news reported both the official and the black-market rates, and that each rate was weighed against the US dollar. I also spoke about my experience in the local supermarket in Goioerê—how the meat and produce were all local, yet locals told me that the choicest selections were shipped to the

US. The article that ran was titled "Williams Amazed at Power of US."*

Although I may have gained insights into the experiences of "race" and racism in Brazil, and may have even bought somewhat into the idea of "progress" in the United States, the power that amazed me was that of US bullying and propaganda. The "promise" of America had found a way of living rent free in the heads of those outside it. The blockbuster films, syndicated TV shows, and output of musicians had tantalized the imaginations of a nation—rich with its own history—so much that, in the late eighties, anywhere I went in Brazil, including school, groups of people would gather around me mainly to ask if what they had heard about the US was true.

Here is what is true: the slaveholder, writer of the Declaration of Independence, and third president of the US, Thomas Jefferson, wholeheartedly believed in the intellectual and aesthetic superiority of white people. He wrote:

> Are not the fine mixtures of red and white, the expressions of every passion by greater or less suffusions of color in the one, preferable to the eternal monotony, which reigns in the countenances, that immoveable veil of black which covers all the

---

* Lee Gittler, "Williams Amazed at Power of US," *Middletown Times Herald Record,* August 1989.

> emotions of the other race? Add to these flowing hair, a more elegant symmetry of form, their own judgment in favor of the whites, declared by their preference of them, as uniformly as is the preference of the Oran-ootan for the black woman over those of his own species. The circumstance of superior beauty, is thought worthy attention in the propagation of our horses, dogs, and other domestic animals; why not in that of man?[9]

Despite his views on the animal-like inferiority of African people, Jefferson is on record as being opposed to slavery. Of interest is this paragraph he originally wrote in his first draft of the US Declaration of Independence:

> He [King George III] has waged a cruel war against human nature itself, violating its most sacred rights of life & liberty in the persons of a distant people who never offended him, captivating & carrying them into slavery in another hemisphere, or to incur miserable death in their transportation thither. This piratical warfare, the opprobrium of *infidel* powers, is the warfare of the CHRISTIAN king of Great Britain.
>
> Determined to keep open a market where MEN should be bought and sold, he has prostituted his negative for suppressing every

> legislative attempt to prohibit or to restrain this execrable commerce.[10]

This paragraph was part of the original draft, delivered by Jefferson and the Committee of Five, who oversaw the task, on June 28, 1776, just seven days before an edited version of the declaration, which removed this paragraph to appease slaveholding representatives from South Carolina and Georgia, was ratified by the Continental Congress, on July 4, 1776.

Here is another truth: the emphasis in US education on African Americans who fought to secure an independent United States clouds the truth of how the promise of freedom made most enslaved Africans in the American colonies root for the defeat of the patriots.[11] And it is in this manner that, since its inception, most American truths have run counter to freedom or liberation for Black and Indigenous people. In the words of Kwame Ture:

> Our problem has been, as Black people, we have always been concerned about white America, never about us. And what we've always thought is that white America equals the same interest as us. That is not true. We must now be concerned with us. Let me give you some examples. We always want to prove what good Americans we are. The very first man to die for the war of

> independence in this country was a Black man named Crispus Attucks. He was a fool. Because here he was fighting for white folks' freedom and millions of his brothers were enslaved in the very [same] country. But we wanted to prove what great Americans we were. We begged the white folks to let us fight in [the Civil War] and they said, "No." So we organized ourselves in bands of armies, training ourselves in our bare feet, to prove to the white folk what great Americans we were. Please let us fight, white folks. And finally they came and inspected our troops and said, "Good nigger. You can fight." And they had us fighting the Indians, like fools. We should have teamed up with the Indians and taken care of you know who.[12]

Ture's assessment feels even more critical now, as a developing Black American middle class, coupled with the hordes of Black Americans still in poverty, struggling against increasingly harsh conditions and diminished rights in the workplace, still hold steadfast to a capitalist indoctrination. The fact that capitalism itself has been shown by scholars, like Cedric Robinson, to be rooted in and beholden to racial exploitation has done little to sway the conversation. In his biography of Paul Robeson, historian Gerald Horne concludes, "Moreover, if Stalin discredited socialism for all time, why didn't the Atlantic Slave Trade discredit capitalism for all time?"[13]

Here I am, all these years later, reflecting on that year in Brazil, what I learned there through the music and through the eyes of people who had been duped by the America-first propaganda on TV. Here I am, still answering the question, "Is it true that America is free?" Over and over, I must name the ways in which America has never been free—and point to the writers, thinkers, and musicians who have taught me to read all the literature like a skeptic.

Chapter Six

Zombification: Losing the Propaganda War

It was at a house party in Fort Greene, Brooklyn, in 1995, that I remember feeling as if we were losing the propaganda war. My compass up to that point had been music. Music had, in many ways, laid the groundwork for a kind of enthusiasm I felt about the direction we were heading as a society and, in particular, as a community. Perhaps every generation feels something like this; yet, for me, witnessing the birth and directionality of hip-hop felt as if we were successfully pushing back against the ideologies being fed us through popular media. It felt as if we had taken it upon ourselves to pass on information we had learned or gathered—not merely in the words and messages in lyrics but also in the beats themselves, unpacked through the dances. I felt like we were unlocking something. And clearly it wasn't only us. By the early to mid-nineties I had begun to dig into jungle, drum 'n' bass, and trip-hop, from the UK, which kinda felt like a game of telephone, where a word was whispered into the ear of the person closest to you and passed around the circle. By the time it finally came back, you were like, "What?!" That's how I felt listening to Tricky's "Nearly God" ("You promised me poems") or Portishead's *Glory Box,* coupled with the complex rhythms of drum 'n' bass, had me feeling like we were on the cusp of something.

Then, in the fall of '94, I happened into a poetry reading and was even more convinced that we were working through complex equations, waking the dead, articulating that which had been in the shadows and under covers for too long, which is to say I was excited.* In my memory, I always return to that house

* I had begun writing poetry in college—in our spare time, my friends and I had formed a collective called Red Clay. We put out a monthly zine, and I contributed essays and poems. Writing poems for the zine helped me realize that when my writing was not for an academic assignment, it seemed to naturally take a poetic form. I wasn't regularly writing poems as a practice yet. In the fall of '94 I began graduate studies at NYU's Tisch School of the Arts for acting. Our instructors insisted that we carry a personal journal every day. They would not be looking at it; they simply wanted to ensure that we were monitoring our insights and growth as we matriculated. Being required to keep a journal on my person at all times (pre-cellphone/smartphone/social media) is what tripped me into documenting my thoughts and ideas on a regular basis. Before that I was not frequenting poetry readings or identifying as a poet.

party, a few blocks from where I lived, in Fort Greene, Brooklyn, at the home of a young hip-hop journalist/filmmaker I had met at the open mic on Friday nights at the Brooklyn Moon Cafe. At these open mics, we were discussing literature, science fiction, gender, our diets, and projecting these poems and conversations into the ether. I had begun carrying a little journal in my back pocket, instead of a wallet, and would pull it out to scribe thoughts whenever inspiration hit. Sometimes that inspiration was when I was reading; other times I'd be on the subway, observing people, but more times than not, the inspiration would come on the dance floor. The energy of the space, the people, the sound, the volume at a level that might as well be headphones, would have me literally spinning, and thoughts would pop up. It didn't hurt that the poetry I was most moved by at that moment was by Sufi poets, like Hafez and Rumi. I was also meditating daily, and in that essence I would also achieve the sort of epiphanies that swirled around me on the dance floor. I made mixtapes that would orchestrate my journey from my house to the subway to school.

My deep dives had taken on much greater proportions since my time in Brazil. I was exploring sound like an archaeologist explores ancient landmarks. Spending hours in the record store, coming home with albums, reading the booklets as I listened. Dissecting the liner notes of old jazz albums, staring at the artwork, anything the artist had to offer. I wasn't making music yet or identifying as a musician, but music, with literature as a constant undercurrent, was where I could see the future. So the Fort Greene house party, which typically I should have enjoyed, threw me for a loop when our host put on a song that had recently come out, which I heard at all times of night from passing cars but had never heard in a club—or, in this case, at a basement party, packed from wall to wall with Brooklyn's finest. The song began, and in one swoop the entire dance floor latched on to the women in the recording, repeating the refrain, "Get Money!,"[1] and the thought that struck was, "Oh fuck, they got us."

It was something about the disproportion of the emphasis. I wasn't paying attention to the verse lyrics; rather, it was, for me, a light shift, like the music was zombifying us. I'd call it a bad trip, but I hadn't taken anything. I was overcome with the feeling of our being enveloped by something we needed to fight against. I had never felt that from music before. I had never caught a glimpse of a future that I didn't look forward to. I began to wonder whether music had the potential of poisoning us. There were very few public intellectuals or philosophers to engage with at the time, and, for many people, rappers had filled that void to confirm our ongoing critique of the programming that was thrust upon us. Again, I am not simply pointing to lyrics or messages in songs but also to the innovation, the flow, the style through which ideas were being unpacked, the packaging itself, the music, the bass, the sampling of ideas from the past, doubling up the drums, rearranging the patterns—it all felt like a process of making sense of our existence while honoring the lessons and teachers, collecting our histories, deconstructing the path. It was proof of life, of counterculture, and resistance. Yet, that night it hit me that the power of the music could trigger different realities. I became more critical. I felt that rappers who bragged about selling crack—after we all knew that the CIA played a role in bringing crack into our communities—were basically bragging about working for the CIA. What's next? We gonna listen to cops rap?*

---

* Don't get me wrong. I was neither a prude nor sheltered. When I came back from Brazil, my best friend had become one of the city's biggest dealers. A lot of people I knew who sold before I left were now working for him. Coke, guns, cars, and lots of cash. I had been surrounded by it before I left for Brazil, and when I came back it was time for the close-up. I was never fazed or judgmental. Most of my friends sold. The fact that I didn't wasn't a big deal to them. We all had hip-hop in common, and everybody knew that I could rap. So, it was all peace. Most of the time I felt these cats were trying to protect me. They never involved me in their beefs. And they had my back if I had any beefs of my own. Now I was acquiring a kind of critical beef with the status quo of where the music was heading—and, as I saw it, thus society. Although I had given up rapping soon

Capitalist intrigue in hip-hop began to feel like a psyop, a successful extension of COINTELPRO. In the run-up to his 1968 election, Richard Nixon was sneaky af when he coopted Black Power into Black capitalism:

> His plan, he assured the public, was in sync with the true spirit of black nationalism: "Black extremists are guaranteed headlines when they shout "burn" or "get a gun," but much of the black militant talk these days is actually in terms far closer to the doctrines of free enterprise than to those of the welfarist '30s." Nixon promised "more black ownership . . . black pride, black jobs, black opportunity, and yes, black power, in the best, the constructive sense of that often misapplied term."[2]

Nixon's plan was to neutralize Black resistance and undermine Black demands for economic redress and reparations by openly touting the idea of Black ownership, entrepreneurship, and a pledge to support small Black businesses. FBI Director J. Edgar

---

after I got back from Brazil, primarily thinking that I was too old, my growing appreciation of poetry and music and my craving for sounds that I wanted to hear put me on a path to create the example of directions I thought we could head, musically, an approach that I found more satisfying than the idea of becoming a critic.

Hoover had stated that same year that the Black Panther Party "without question, represents the greatest threat to the internal security of the country."[3] That threat was not simply because the revolutionary organization, with its black guns and berets, symbolized Black Power, but because the Marxist-Leninist teachings the Panthers followed had inspired them to join forces with other revolutionary groups to build a coalition of power that connected white, Indigenous, Mexican, Puerto Rican, South Asian, East Asian, and West Asian* communities. The Black Panthers' slogan was "Power to the People!"

Nixon saw this movement as an actual threat, and his plan to spread the gospel of black capitalism and encourage Black people to invest in their own communities, under the pretense of "People who own their homes don't burn down their neighborhoods," was embraced by conservatives as a form of voluntary segregation.

> Nelson Rockefeller's strategist called the concept "a stroke of political genius," and Rockefeller himself supported the idea. *National Review* editor William F. Buckley praised the "spirit" of "militant black leaders who have been preaching black initiative, black capitalism, and yes, black

---

* The descriptor "Middle East" assumes the British Empire as the center of the world.

> power." Buckley aligned black capitalism with a libertarian small-government philosophy, stating that Black Power was allied with conservatives in their fight against "that huge monster on the banks of the Potomac." Buckley proposed that the still-undefined program need not involve the entire black populace, because "scattered success can give universal hope."[4]

Once in office, Nixon created the Office of Minority Business Enterprise within the Department of Commerce, which was allocated $0. Then, through the Small Business Act, he allocated $66 million in federal contracts to "minority"-owned firms, which amounted to less than 0.1 percent of the $76 billion dollars in federal contracts that year.[5] The Equal Employment Opportunity Commission, which had been created by the 1964 Civil Rights Act, introduced affirmative action to encourage businesses to hire more Black employees. The terms were voluntary yet with an open record and measurement of the voluntary goals. Nixon enacted these plans as a means of dismantling his Democratic predecessor Lyndon B. Johnson's "War on Poverty," aka the Economic Opportunity Act, which had established forty programs aimed at eliminating poverty by improving living conditions for residents of low-income neighborhoods and helping the poor access economic opportunities—a mission that generations of civil rights activists had fought, and some even given their lives, for.

Of course, the overall impact of these policies of the Nixon administration* would eventually be felt in how many more people—and, notably, artists—would self-identify as or aspire to be "businessmen" or "entrepreneurs."† On one hand was the desire of artists to no longer be taken advantage of, as previous

* Pushing Black capitalism was only one prong of Nixon's attack on Black radicals and leftists, who had successfully mobilized youth across the nation to stand up to US imperialism abroad and fascism at home. The second prong replaced Johnson's War on Poverty with a "War on Drugs." Twenty-five years later, Nixon's domestic affairs advisor, White House counsel, and Watergate coconspirator, John Ehrlichman, set the record straight: "The Nixon campaign in 1968, and the Nixon White House after that, had two enemies: the antiwar left and Black people. You understand what I'm saying? We knew we couldn't make it illegal to be either against the war or Black, but by getting the public to associate the hippies with marijuana and Blacks with heroin, and then criminalizing both heavily, we could disrupt those communities. We could arrest their leaders, raid their homes, break up their meetings, and vilify them night after night on the evening news. Did we know we were lying about the drugs? Of course we did." Dan Baum, "Legalize It All," *Harper's* magazine, April 2016.

† In a way, the encouraging of entrepreneurship is another way of dismantling solidarity in the workplace, of union busting (or union starvation), pitting artists against each other.

generations had been. On another was the dream—for some—of being able to take advantage of fame or popularity and leverage it into a clothing or alcohol brand, never really offering a critique of those industries in terms of exploitation of workers in sweatshops, or the inflated pricing of celebrity brands, rather envisioning a seat at the table, a chance to exploit.

My critique of capitalism found its way into my earliest poems and even into my raps beforehand. A cocktail of what I read, sensed, experienced, and imagined began to take shape in poems like "Amethyst Rocks," in which, inspired by Chuck D's "Hustler of Culture" verse in *Welcome to the Terrordome,* I imagined myself dealing crystals that enhanced self-realization. "I stand on the corner of the block, slinging amethyst rocks. . ." I began to understand that hip-hop was not some victorious battle in which we, with a sound and language of protest, had successfully broken through the cracks of a system built against us, but that hip-hop, like us, could be—had already been—co-opted into the system. As I say in my first single, recorded with Rick Rubin, on my first album, *Amethyst Rock Star,* "How much will it cost to buy you out of buying into a reality that originally bought you . . . a dime a dozen?" and "What have you bought into? How much will it cost to buy you out?"

When people argue that it is useless to point to the many horrors of the past, that we must "let bygones be bygones," they are falling into the trap of thinking that settler-colonial and imperial "progress" has pushed humanity forward, rather than acknowledging the social movements that forced governing powers to concede. So, when Fela Kuti says, "Music is the weapon of the future," or Nina Simone says, "An artist's responsibility is to speak to the times," it's important that you know what time it is—and don't let these mfs set the clock back. A weaponized music crosses borders without passports. It can serve to uplift and inspire mass movements. It can serve as reminder of the possibilities authoritarian power would have us forget.

Meanwhile, art—cinema and TV, in particular—that propagates the idea of heroism (or stokes fear of "terrorism") and reinforces a belief in the veritability of the state, or of "Western civilization," runs the risk of lulling the viewer deeper into the throes of indoctrination. Zombification, in other words. If that is the idea of entertainment, then art is allowing its power to be co-opted by an existing system. Unquestioned realities purported to be truths become the foundation of thought; thus, the task of unlearning becomes more entangled and complex. What may feel like a natural unfolding of events is often far from natural—more often than not, it is a regurgitation of a past that has been intentionally kept from public knowledge or discourse, as evidenced by much of what we see in the news today, whether regarding migrants, xenophobia, colonial discourse over the rights of Indigenous groups, the reversing of landmark decisions that secured women's right to abortion, or restricting corporate money in elections. Our current juncture raises a critical question: If "art" can be used to trigger such a strategic conservative/autocratic response—endowing corporations with power that in a "democracy" should be in the hands of the people—why can't the people use art to trigger the strategic responses to take that power back?

Let's look at how art and propaganda propelled one of the most powerful and destructive changes that has happened in our lifetime. The 2010 *Citizens United v. the Federal Election Commission* (FEC) Supreme Court decision changed campaign finance laws in the US by determining that laws restricting the political spending of corporations and unions are inconsistent with the free speech clause of the First Amendment.[6] The lawsuit was originally filed in response to the release of filmmaker Michael Moore's 2004 documentary *Fahrenheit 9/11*. Citizens United, an organization funded by conservative billionaires who had been working behind the scenes for decades to cement a larger role in US politics, filed a complaint with the FEC, arguing that the film's publicity campaign—which was strongly critical of the Bush-Cheney administration—constituted political advertising. Thus, according to the 2002 Bipartisan Campaign Reform Act (BCRA), they argued, the film's publicity could not be aired within the thirty days before a primary election or sixty days before a general election. The FEC dismissed the complaint. Citizens United responded by making its own documentary, *Celsius 41.11*, that was critical of Moore's documentary and of the Democratic Party candidate, John Kerry.[7] The FEC decided that airing *Celsius 41.11* and its advertising was in violation of the Federal Election Campaign Act because Citizens United was not an actual film production company. So, in 2008, Citizens United readied a new documentary called *Hillary: The Movie*, planning to run ads during the primary season and then air it on DirecTV. The FEC determined that this film was in violation of BCRA constraints on "electioneering communication" by mentioning a candidate within sixty days of a general election or thirty days of a primary and prohibited from expenditures by corporations and labor unions—thus preventing *Hillary: The Movie* from being broadcast. Citizens United appealed the FEC's decision in the US District Court for the District of Columbia; after the District Court's ruling that advertisements for *Hillary: The Movie* could be aired but not the film, they appealed the decision to the US Supreme Court.[8]

In an infamous decision, issued on January 24, 2010, the Supreme Court ruled 5–4 in favor of Citizens United, stating that the sections of the BCRA that prohibited independent political spending on "electioneering communications" by corporations and unions violated the First Amendment clause protecting freedom of speech.[9] In common terms, the Roberts Supreme Court decided that corporations and unions count as people under the US Constitution, and that money equals speech. It also decided—although this was not the intent of the lawsuit—that cynical, bad-faith deployment of an art form was beside the point; that, in fact, art itself was beside the point; money is the point; money is speech; money speaks loudest.

Now, if you're anything like me, you saw the Moore doc back in 2004 and thought, "Perfect timing." Yet, such liberal half-measures that hold up the American exceptionalist narrative will not get us over the finish line, to true Black liberation, which includes abolition, and Land Back for Indigenous people. Persistent investment in, and insistence on, the so-called promise of America excuses its original sin by continuing to overlook the Indigenous dispossessed:

> "Tribal sovereignty" is not possible while colonial authority exists, and perhaps a more pressing concern is that it is fundamentally a colonial political concept. While calls to "honor the treaties" on one hand could be viewed as assertions of Indigenous political authority, on the other, they are a myopic urge to revisit forced negotiations

> made under duress to benefit the colonial order. The strategy of colonial expansion was not designed to sustain treaties with Peoples that invaders planned to assimilate into their order. The U.S. government had absolutely no problem breaking every treaty it marked its name on. From the colonizer's perspective treaties were always temporary; they were a concession to captivity, an agreement to civilization.[10]

As the Diné musician and author Klee Benally wrote in his brilliant essay "Unknowable: Against an Indigenous Anarchist Theory," nature negates the state.[11] Look at our current state. How much more do we need to see? These mfs are against nature, against a woman's bodily sovereignty, against the migration that is a direct result of their imperialist government destabilization practices, against an honest analysis of history or transparency in the present, against any modicum of restraint in regard to the rivers, the ocean, the climate, against affordable access to healthcare or education, against using our own tax money to secure the basic necessities for our survival, and most definitely against any acquired awareness that tells us our lives need not be as stressful, that our individualist scope of survival is also an indoctrination, that there are people, communities, and countries that marvel at the cutthroat realities of our existence, who cough once and go straight to the doctor to see what's up, without any thought of what it will cost them, not because they are rich but because their government is not actually banking on their death or incarceration, who don't understand how a "private" hospital or health insurance or "credit history" works, who can't believe what we put up with for a chance at the lottery of success, who can make no sense of how we have no access to all that we should have access to. And then there are those who have never lived without a US sanction restricting their diet or livelihood, who have only known American mercenaries and charities, who face restrictions on the seeds they can plant, who are subject to policies we could not fathom, imposed by a corporate "superpower," who are described as "terrorists" or "countless," as in simply not counting, whose children are listed as casualties when they are killed in their favorite Spiderman pajamas, who are under constant threat by weapons that read "Made in USA," who find it difficult to imagine that we are unaware, and may prefer the clarity of thinking that we simply don't care, who feel no difference between our Republican and Democratic presidents and congresspeople, as they are fed by the same ruthless corporations that furnish the local militias and overseers that enslave their children to mine the resources that should be the wealth of their land yet remain its curse, who are subject to weapon, medical, agricultural, and anthropological experiments, who wish that America would mind its own mf business, who know many aspects of our own country's history better than we do. And it's not just the US, it's England, Belgium, France, Portugal, Spain, Italy, Germany. What America did was merge the European idea of colonialism with the British practice of capitalism, and free it from its boundaries and disputed limitations. America industrialized it, digitized it, and sold it back to the highest bidder, having already set the price. That is the only freedom America knows and practices. The rest is propaganda that will be used to feed your apathetic zombification while enforcing the surveillance mechanisms of the carceral state. America is not something to be won back. It must surrender.

Chapter Seven

Where Poetry Led Me to Protest

In 2023, my first film, *Slam*,* was scheduled to be screened in Brazil in celebration of its twenty-fifth anniversary. Twenty-five years earlier, in 1998, I had returned to Brazil for the first time since my teenage exchange year for *Slam*'s South American premiere, at the Rio de Janeiro International Film Festival. On that trip, I gave my first poetry reading in Brazil and met a fast-growing generation of young Brazilian poets, mostly Indigenous and Black. Since then, the popularity of poetry slams and "spoken word" has

* *Slam* was the first feature narrative directed by (otherwise) documentarian Marc Levin. It was shot primarily in a DC jail with actual prisoners as actors and follows Raymond Joshua (played by me) as he moves through the prison-industrial complex after being apprehended with weed. I was hired as a screenwriter and eventually cast as the lead during my third year at NYU. *Slam* won the 1998 Grand Jury Prize at the Sundance Film Festival and the 1998 Caméra d'Or prize at the Cannes Film Festival.

brought a new wave of poets—in Brazil and around the world—to the cultural fore and, with them, much-needed dialogue (and inspired monologues) on the realities faced and worlds imagined by a new generation of voices.

In October 2023, I again found myself in Rio de Janeiro, this time attending an annual literary festival in Brazil's oldest favela, Providencia. While I was there, news broke of a prison escape and attacks in Occupied Palestine. It was my third time being invited to Festa Literarias das Periferias (FLUP), held in Rio's favelas since 2012. Brazil had been through its own political upheaval since my last visit, in November 2018. That year, the festival was held in Pequena África, the neighborhood that became the home of thousands of freed slaves between 1850 and 1920. I was the featured poet at the festival's international poetry slam, which featured poets from more than forty different countries, including several from the African continent, more than eighty poets from across Brazil, and the Slam do Corpo (Body Slam), where deaf poets recited their poems in sign language. The festival's theme that year was "Negritude"; the poetry was hard-hitting in response to the fact that a month earlier, on October 7, 2018, followed by a runoff, the far-right presidential candidate Jair Bolsonaro, who opposed abortion, affirmative action, same-sex marriage, drug legalization, and more, had been elected president.

When I first started touring the US as a poet, it felt as if we had handed a gift to English and literature teachers across the country who were looking for thoughtful and exciting ways of engaging their classrooms. How often I met students, told to attend a reading as an assignment or for extra credit, surprised to learn I wasn't much older than they were. And, always, a smattering of teachers, drinks in hand yet soberly earnest in their appreciation. We poets knew that we had awakened something by reminding a generation already strung out on hip-hop that poetry didn't belong to the dead. That beyond the beats and bars—which were prisons and prisms—we were also contemplating our relationships to gender and social constructs/contracts, questioning the colonial parameters of contagion and design, while challenging the ever-changing face of technology through the recognition that there will always be new life immersed in this art form older than recorded time.*

---

* I took the attention afforded me carefully, always reading more than I wrote. I never considered myself having traveled someplace if I had not personally entered someone's kitchen. I mined my emotions through heartbreak, fatherhood, loss, the miraculous, all forms of love, and continued to let music guide me. I had promised myself, in my twenty-third year, to always remain a student. Always more to learn. As with my first love, acting, I fell in love with the process. In truth, I hesitated to refer to myself as a poet in the first decade of writing. It felt dishonest.

Poetry served as a passport for me into not only Brazil's favelas but also into South African townships, Indigenous reservations, Aboriginal community centers, French and US prisons, juvenile facilities, halfway houses, high schools, countless universities, and prestigious venues across the world. The reality was that the words and thoughts shared in small New York City cafés in the mid- to late nineties and onward were in direct conversation with words and thoughts being shared in other cities and towns across the world. We all saw poetry as a useful tool to deconstruct a toxic relationship with unwarranted realities and definitions of existence. Yet, exist we do, and the world, beyond audience, must reckon with it.

I remember thinking, during the candidacy of Barack Obama, and later during Black Lives Matter uprisings, how many of the topics and poems that had shaken poetry readings a decade earlier had entered the public lexicon and the language of social movements, then, subsequently, were incorporated and co-opted by political platforms and parties. This has been

---

It was true that I wrote poetry, yet being called a poet felt too much like a compliment for me to turn and call myself one. I wasn't certain I had read, studied, or even experienced enough. For me, it was never absolutely the love of language; rather, language felt inadequate, like it would need to be hot-wired to achieve something worthy of interrupting the music. I wasn't interested in filling silences. I adored them. But then, I also love an overgrown garden.

the trajectory of many radical ideologies and serves as a means of defanging all possibilities of revolt, perpetually leading people back into the existing political framework. It would not be fair to say that the purpose of these poetry readings and slams had been to instigate a social revolution, yet the pooling of thoughts and energies carried a transformative optimism that the future would eventually fall into the right hands, that people were thinking, critiquing, studying, and working toward articulating a clearer grasp on what it would take for the world we know to become the world we imagine. Many of these people were already teachers, organizers, activists, living in shared environments, squats, were part of cooperatives and communes, providing services and mutual aid, situating their work in disenfranchised communities, like the poets behind the poetry festival I was attending in Brazil.

The Obama era served to more deeply entrench Black people in the belief that the system could be reformed from the inside. The modus operandi of his campaign was "Hope," which had immediately struck me as something to be wary of, as I had spent years meditating on a translation of the thirteenth verse of the Tao Te Ching, which states:

> Success is as dangerous as failure. Hope is as hollow as fear.

> What does it mean that success is as dangerous as failure? Whether you go up the ladder or down it, your position is shaky. When you stand with your two feet on the ground, you will always keep your balance.
>
> What does it mean that hope is as hollow as fear? Hope and fear are both phantoms that arise from thinking of the self. When we don't see the self as self, what do we have to fear?
>
> See the world as your self. Have faith in the way things are. Love the world as your self; then you can care for all things.[1]

It was the idea of hope being as hollow as fear that stuck with me. The year of Obama's election, I released an album titled *The Inevitable Rise and Liberation of Niggy Tardust,* based on my observation at the time of what Kwame Ture might term "scientific socialism"—that as surely as capitalism would inevitably lead to fascism, the only path to a just society that honored Indigenous sovereignty and learning, and made all the necessary transformations to ensure the well-being of all people—workers, children, the elderly—along with the earth and the preservation of nature, would inevitably be one in which the people demanded socialism.

Yet, the Obama presidency amounted to putting a Black face on American imperialism, while enticing

Black people with the promise that you, too, can be an avatar of US leadership . . . as long as you don't get in the way of the money, the land grabs, the drone strikes, the coups d'etat, and the destabilization games necessary to make sure that we (America) inherit Earth.

▼

As news spread of what was happening in Occupied Palestine, I was not alone in my concern. I sat with other attendees, over lunch, with the revolving question of how the entity would respond. We knew that it would be brutal but held on to the belief that they would somehow be reined back by other world powers. The fact that the Hannibal Directive, as more than mere conspiracy, had been triggered and executed without any mainstream media coverage or confirmation indicated clearly that something much crueler was in the works.

I regret to admit that I visited Occupied Palestine, in 2010, after reluctantly accepting an invitation by a collective of young anarchist Jews I had met online, all of whom had found individual and roundabout ways of not serving in the IOF.* I accepted the invitation on the one condition that they would take me into Palestine, where they said they were very actively working

* Israeli Occupation Forces.

with Palestinian activists. I was unaware of the Boycott, Divestment, Sanctions call to artists to boycott the entity when I agreed to go. Once I learned of the BDS call, I held on to the arrogant belief that poetry was different. That it held the power to turn the entity on itself and shatter its supremacist illusions. That was the dumb shit I was on. My stubbornness won me front-row seats to first-class discrimination. The apartheid wall, "Israeli Only" freeways, indoctrinated youth who believed they were surrounded by enemies, armed with machine guns. The memories of that trip hit me in the stomach with absolute disgust.*

---

* When I arrived, I strolled toward customs with my guitar on my back, as a friend had advised me to do, "to avoid suspicion." A man in a suit aggressively pulled me aside and asked what the hell I was doing there. I thought it was funny but kept my cool. I'd had my share of aggressive customs agents and had grown to enjoy the blank look that came over their face when I responded, "A poetry reading." A statement loaded with contraband, I surrender. He looked at me like maybe he had the same thought. I was sure it wasn't my good looks that made him pull me aside, yet I hadn't even been asked to show my passport, which, as a US citizen, I figured, would be good as gold. After he demanded it, he thumbed through it and froze: "Who do you know in Morocco?" I answered, "A few poets." He held eye contact, but I've always won at that. He kept thumbing through the passport and froze again: "What were you doing in Turkey?" I motioned at the guitar on my shoulder, "Concerts?" A few staring contests later, I finally made it through customs and met my host, who pulled

over to a small kiosk as soon as we exited airport grounds and asked if I'd like a shot. Turns out that was the number one question I was asked with every new encounter, minus the one girl in the collective who explained that everybody their age stayed high to avoid thinking about their time in the IOF. The vibes were strange, and I never felt comfortable. I was shocked to see American franchises like KFC and Pizza Hut all over the place.

The poetry reading was that night. The venue was sold out and overcrowded. Unlike most instances, where I'm prone to wander the streets, explore, get lost, meet people, I stayed backstage until it was time to go on. Two poems I remember reading were "Children of the Night," which to me is more like a spell to enchant the space and rework the energy of a room, and a few long excerpts of "said the shotgun to the head." In both cases, I had the impression that these poems were fine-tuned for the situation and whom I was speaking to. The audience was rabid, yet I couldn't escape the feeling that this was also in response to anyone from the outside world coming to visit them. I felt gross. I retreated back to the rundown house where a few members of the collective lived and stayed up late listening to stories about how they began seeing through their indoctrination, the tricks they used to avoid serving in the military, and their active participation in the weekly nonviolent protests in Bil'in, the nearby Palestinian village of about two thousand residents that we would be visiting in the morning.

What I was clear on is that they had all been indoctrinated since their youth with cartoons, media, and religious and political leaders all telling them that they were surrounded by enemies who wanted them dead, and that it was their duty to fight for their country. In appearance, they reminded me of the straggly hippie kids I met in poetry readings in northern California and Oregon, though slightly less patchouli-oriented and less removed from their settler-hood.

The next morning, we set out early for Bil'in, where I was to meet Iyad Burnat, the Palestinian organizer of the Bil'in Popular Committee Against the Wall and Settlement, who led the weekly protests that had begun in 2005, after the IOF removed a thousand olive trees to construct the West Bank Barrier, aka the Wall of Apartheid, which stretches for 440 miles. The International Criminal Court issued an advisory opinion in 2004, finding that the barrier qualifies as a violation of international law. In 2003, the UN General Assembly adopted a resolution that charged the entity's building of the wall as a violation of international law and demanded its removal. It has not been removed. In Bil'in, the wall separated local farmers from their farmland, diminishing roughly 60 percent of the village's territory. Burnat and fellow activists won a minor victory in 2007 when the entity's high court ruled that the wall unnecessarily interfered with the residents without offering any "security advantage." Yet, in 2010 the wall had yet to be removed. I would also be meeting a number of local villagers and activists, including members of the Abu Rahmah family, whose son and brother, Bassem, had been killed a year earlier, at one of the weekly nonviolent protests, when he was shot in the chest with an (illegal) teargas cannister.

Leaving the city, my host slowed down to translate the sign at the entrance to the freeway: "Israeli Only." We drove less than an hour before pulling off and encountering a military checkpoint. Four teenage-looking soldiers with machine guns approached the car. They exchanged a few words with my host, and we moved on. Within moments we were in a completely different world. Two barefoot children ran behind a donkey cart. The road was dusty, small houses were makeshift, and the people were brown. Robes, sandals, trees, sheep—I had gone from a city that looked like a worn-down Miami to suddenly being in what felt like a truly ancient land. As we approached a village, I watched a group of kids playing soccer in flip-fops and bare feet in a large open field. The car slowed, and a young man approached the car. Noticing my watching the kids play, he called one of the kids over and told him to bring the ball. The ball was made of hundreds of rubber bands wrapped around an object. He pulled a handful of the rubber bands to the side, and beneath it all was a spent teargas cannister shaped like a grenade. He motioned me closer and told me to look closely at the small print: Made in USA. "It's illegal but they still shoot it," he said, pointing to the high wall that snaked across the hill overlooking the field. I hadn't noticed it until it was impossible not to notice. The wall was topped with barbed wire and seemed to stretch on forever. "Welcome to Palestine."

We went inside the building where the meeting was to take place and learned that half the people expected to be there would probably not be showing up, as the village had been raided at 4 a.m. that morning and some people were still detained. A British activist, who was staying in the building as an international observer, had been thrown from his wheelchair. The IOF had been conducting raids at all times of night for the past week, which was their common method of fucking with them, to try to throw them off their routine of weekly meetings and protests. People slowly trickled in, and over the course of a few hours I was given the rundown on nonviolent protests in Bil'in and other nearby villages also protesting the illegal wall and settlements in construction on the hills above them. The Bil'in protests had gained attention because they chose weekly themes, actions, and sometimes costumes, and had encouraged activists from the entity and from the international community to participate, to bring worldwide attention to the illegal actions being conducted by the entity and the overall struggle of Palestinian people. Eventually, they asked if I wanted to see the wall. A handful of us left the building and began walking on the dirt path beside the field, up the hill toward the wall. I noted the grass was littered with teargas cannisters, like pinecones. A kid ran up and showed me a rubber bullet. One of the group noticed activity from two soldiers, standing on top of a military jeep with rifles pointed our direction. We stayed put for a few minutes; they showed me the grove where they had once all tied themselves to trees, and eventually said, "I think we should go back."

The next day we were back on the "Israeli Only" freeway, driving to Jerusalem. My first thought as we approached was that it kinda looked like Beverly Hills. My host was there to dig at a record store for a party he was DJing that night, and I decided to wander alone. I walked toward the walls of the old city. The closer I got, the more soldiers with machine guns I saw. I remember noting it was a Sunday and businesses were open, kids were in school uniforms. It felt like an American Monday. I couldn't get past the police state of it all. I entered the gates, and it was a marketplace surrounding all the ancient sites, selling T-shirts with pictures of Osama Bin Laden with a target on his head, Obama, Jesus, and American fighter jets. It was a lot.

The thought of flipping those tables over had to have crossed somebody's mind. Maybe that's what all the IOF soldiers were on guard to prevent. People with loudspeakers were saying shit like, "Would the Mount of Olive congregation from Fort Worth please meet in front of the Church of the Holy Sepulcher?" I was in no state to appreciate the relics of antiquity as I was quite literally overcome with disgust by the blend of American tourism, and the entity's militarism. Pure occupation.

I made my way back to the record store. As my host was loading the car up with vinyl, I saw a dude in shorts, Timberlands, and a hockey jersey, with his cap cocked to the side, walking like he was strolling down Pitkin Avenue in Brooklyn. As he got closer, I saw he was clearly Palestinian; we made eye contact, shared a nod; he reached out and gave me pound and said softly, "My nigga," and kept it moving. Tone, inflection, and homeboy's confidence was so on point, it hit like manna from heaven, erasing all the discomfort and anger I had been feeling . . . for the moment.

My host was spinning a reggae set at a venue not far from the hotel I'd be staying at that night before flying out early the next morning. White boys with locks on the dance floor. I had never really thought about the number of times Rastas shout out "the children of Israel" in their music. Obviously, they were not referencing the rowdy kids I saw losing their shit every time those words came through the speakers. I had truly had enough. I walked back to my hotel and counted three instances of Arab kids being stopped and frisked by the police. If seeing is believing, I had certainly seen enough.

I had also spent the previous ten years researching, writing, and spending considerable time with survivors of the Rwandan genocide against the Tutsi, and their children. I knew the stories of how the UN and the Clinton administration had squandered an opportunity to stop it before it happened. I knew firsthand accounts of survivors who, in their most desperate moments, questioned whether the world knew or cared what was happening. I remembered watching CNN with my college roommates, in 1994, and seeing a brief "matter-of-fact" report about what was happening in Rwanda, no longer than two or three sentences, that was followed by a longwinded report of how it might endanger the gorillas, who risked extinction, suddenly delivered with heartfelt concern. The lack of interest in African people was so blatant that the room ignited in an uproar.

Now, in mid-October 2023, I was heading home to a wife who had lost her mother and siblings in the Rwandan genocide and whose ears pricked up at the zoological slurs being used to describe Palestinians by the entity's leadership and spokespeople. Like many genocide scholars, she understood it immediately as a clear warning and trigger. In the words of Frantz Fanon:

> Sometimes the Manichaeanism reaches its logical conclusion and dehumanizes the colonized

> subject. In plain talk, he is reduced to the state of an animal. And consequently, when the colonist speaks of the colonized he uses zoological terms. Allusion is made to the slithery movements of the yellow race, the odors from the "native" quarters, to the hordes, the stink, the swarming, the seething, and the gesticulations. In his endeavors at description and finding the right word, the colonist refers constantly to the bestiary.*

As I returned to Los Angeles, news of the entity's retaliation and the high number of Palestinian casualties began to develop. Online, there was clearly a shift in awareness taking place among a younger generation for whom anticolonial studies and openly performative gestures, like land acknowledgments and the removal of colonial statues, had, at least, helped lay a groundwork better suited to understand the reality of this unfolding scenario. The commonly used Zionist explanation of its being "a complex situation" was quickly rebutted with "It's not complex, it's colonial."

What was unnerving was that many of the same people who had participated in these performative anticolonial gestures, who were knowledgeable of anticolonial movements on the continent and openly supported Indigenous environmental activists at

---

* Frantz Fanon, *The Wretched of the Earth* (Grove Press, 1963).

home, were some of the same people claiming "complexity" in relation to Palestine. This hit me personally, as I began to see names of people I had worked closely with, in film, literature, and music, commenting affirmatively beneath the blatantly anti-Palestinian, anti-Arab, and Islamophobic social media posts of Zionist celebrities, journalists, and influencers or sharing content like "Free Gaza from Hamas." It was startling to me that people who prided themselves on the attention they paid antiracist teachings and behavior had not made the simple step of connecting it to their idea of "a Jewish homeland." When confronted, they would quickly respond that they were anti-Occupation, anti-apartheid, and anti–Netanyahu regime. Yet, it was not the Netanyahu regime that had installed the Occupation or apartheid. The cognitive dissonance was somehow justified because this was "personal"; a grandmother or other relative had fled Europe for Occupied Palestine, and it had grown to represent some sort of heartwarming safe space for them. But at the cost of what? At the expense of whom? European antisemitism was not being refuted, but why were Indigenous Palestinians being made to pay for European crimes? Furthermore, there was a vocalized dismay at Black Americans' "turning their backs" on Jewish "allies" who had just finished marching against the dehumanization of Black Americans by US police, as if this allyship were somehow transactional. To which my response was simply that we are against injustice everywhere. Whatever abuse I, or my ancestry, may have suffered at the hand of my oppressors does not give me the right to oppress others. That's not how it works.

This was how D. W. Griffith had portrayed the period of Reconstruction in *Birth of a Nation.* White actors in Blackface played out an imaginary tale of Blacks in political power, suddenly disenfranchising whites.

> Their corruption and greed are boundless: the law, the courts, the legislature (scenes of the Black-dominated State House are titled "The Riot in the Master's Hall"), the land and real property, social equality, and the most virtuous of white women. Fascinating for its unintended irony, Griffith constructs the indictment of Blacks in a mirror image of the antebellum slave order: fraud and injustice at the polls ("All blacks are given the ballot, while the leading whites are disfranchised"); racial dominion over the law ("The case was tried before a negro magistrate and the verdict rendered against the whites by the negro jury"); the forging of race privileges in legislation ("Passage of a bill, providing for the intermarriage of blacks and whites"); physical terror ("The town given over to crazed negroes brought in by

Lynch and Stoneman to overawe the whites"); the routine and public displays of petty racial humiliation and insult, and so on.[2]

My wife, Anisia, and I watched a documentary called *Tantura*, which interviewed the living perpetrators of the massacre of Palestinians in the village of Tantura in 1948, in the founding of "Israel." One of the perpetrators reflected fondly on how empowering it was to exit a camp in Germany, then be given a gun to release all the animosity and anger they felt by shooting and raping Palestinians. The documentary also covered how the thesis written by the "Israeli" student who originally conducted these interviews was removed from the university archives. And how the student, now an old man, was sued by the murderers, forced by the university to retract his thesis, and ostracized for the rest of his life for trying to make the terroristic crimes of the Occupation's founding common knowledge.[3] But, if you read the writings of Palestinian historians and scholars, these crimes were already common knowledge, with many living survivors and firsthand accounts. This discounting of Palestinian historians and scholars is in line with the numerous Black American, Caribbean, South American, and African scholars whose work was discredited by Europeans and later fell into the hands of European intellectuals, who then recounted the same histories and became the "authorities" on the matter. This is the twisted logic of white supremacy in academia, which, as a history and then philosophy major in undergrad, I knew had damaging repercussions in relation to the ideas of "authority" and "credibility" and the dictates of who controls the narrative. Meanwhile, legacy media, like *The New York Times,* was using its standing to parrot the easily disputed lies by the US and the Occupation governments about crimes committed by the anticolonial resistance, while also proselytizing on their behalf, magnifying blatantly false explanations for why massacres committed by the IOF were necessary or were innocent mistakes.

The litmus test was now, very clearly, people's ability or willingness to make a connection that infringed on their personal feelings about a matter they were closely linked to, and/or to overcome an ideological indoctrination fermented by years of propaganda against "Arab terrorists" and the maligning of Islam as "a breeding ground for terrorism." Beyond that was the anxiety many people experienced upon witnessing and understanding what was happening, yet fearing repercussions for speaking out, because people in leadership roles in their jobs and professions were now openly Zionist. Even the sitting president of the United States, Joseph A. Biden, was very vocally doubling down on his position as a Zionist.

This should have come as little surprise from a man who was also a great friend of segregationists, such as Jesse Helms, and delivered the eulogy for renowned racist Strom Thurmond. As a senator, in 1977, Biden openly worried that desegregation policies would force his children to grow up in "a racial jungle"[4] and opened the doors for other liberal Democrats to side with conservative Republicans against federally mandated integration. That Biden's vice presidency under Obama served to whitewash his legacy has a parallel in the way Obama put a charismatic Black face on US imperialism. The meanings of Zionism and imperialism seemed to be the most necessary to unpack for those who had not previously considered them, an unpacking that many liberals found difficult to face because it put the Democratic Party on the same tier as the Republican Party and challenged their own internalized programming on American exceptionalism. That Democratic leadership stood squarely behind the president, who lied about seeing beheaded babies to manufacture consent for the IOF's genocidal aggression—while, in his political career, he had been the leading recipient of funds from the American Israel Public Affairs Committee (AIPAC)—served as the "mask-off" moment that worked to the advantage of those, like myself, who felt it was necessary for people to understand that both political parties operated under the same racist ideologies that knowingly sacrificed Black and brown lives for US international dominance and greed. And that this dominance and greed were not byproducts of capitalism but rooted in the very history of capitalism itself.

There was a clear gap in understanding between people who received news from traditional outlets and those who had direct access to actual Palestinians, on the ground, via social media. Furthermore, Palestinian journalists, poets, artists, scholars, lawyers, thinkers, influencers, and, in general, all who had grown up as Palestinian were well aware of what many others were just realizing: that their stories would not be carried by mainstream media. Suddenly, it seemed, Palestinian communicators had created a makeshift online university where you could unlearn all the propaganda you had been taught, in byte-size units. The grand unlearning had begun.

People were also sharing information on what was happening in the Democratic Republic of the Congo and Sudan, all linked to the US and its allies' corporate enterprises. The roles of billionaire investors and big tech proved as harmful as the weapons and oil industries. When I posted a thread that included an image of the "Israeli" billionaire Dan Gertler—whose companies owned a controlling share of diamond, cobalt, copper, and oil mines in the DRC, who had been sanctioned by the US and IMF for corrupt practices

("We want our cut!"), who was a major investor in the Occupation's settlements and "security," and whose grandfather, a Romanian Jewish immigrant to the Occupation, had been the president and cofounder of the Israeli Diamond Exchange, notoriously linked to the bartering of South African diamonds in exchange for Israeli weapons during South African apartheid[5]—I received a blistering text from a "friend" with whom we had broken bread several times over the years. For them, my post was the final straw, as they had been holding their tongue for a few weeks, but now my blatant antisemitism was apparent in my posting the photo of Gertler, who, they argued, bore resemblance to the cartoon caricatures used by antisemites to depict Jews. While it was true that Gertler did kind of look like the racist caricature that they sent as proof, I had posted an actual photo from the *Wall Street Journal*. I couldn't help how the dude looked. Yet, what was being overlooked was that, in the thread I posted, we were drawing a direct line between the genocide in Gaza, ongoing atrocities in the DRC, and the Occupation's history in supporting South African apartheid, along with arming other genocidaires and militant groups on the continent.

> Israel is considered one of the most important countries that import rough diamonds, and the most prominent countries that export polished

> diamonds. Most of these diamonds come from African countries such as South Africa, Liberia, Congo, Ivory Coast among others. These countries are directly linked to groups committing massacres against civilians in order to obtain diamonds, and trade with these diamonds leads to the death of tens of thousands of people annually in the countries of origin. The sale and export of these diamonds are linked to major arms deals, the creation of civil wars and financing the fighting groups. This has caused the diamond trade in Africa to be called the dirty trade, the jewels are called "blood diamonds" because the blood of thousands of Africans is shed in order to extract and market them.[6]

Diamonds remain the Occupation's largest export, comprising nearly 30 percent of the entity's gross national income, with the US the number one buyer.[7] Gertler was not the only player; there are many, and I had devoted a considerable amount of my time over the past decade to this kind of information, particularly around the mining of cobalt and coltan, as I was researching to write *Neptune Frost,* the science fiction musical I codirected with my wife and creative partner, Anisia Uzeyman. Wanting to get the story and context right in a work that centered coltan miners, in a land cursed by its richness and ripe with the scars of genocides, recognized and unrecognized, had required a tremendous amount of reading and time on the continent, visiting sites, talking to people, and gathering information.

It's fair to say that over the course of that process, I had become an "investigative poet." And this had somehow prepared me for the moment. The main difference was that now, instead of reading and taking notes, letting information marinate, writing songs or poems inspired by findings, I was compelled to share my thoughts and notes in real time. I began sharing information online as a daily practice. Mostly, I boosted the writings and posts of Palestinians on the ground and across the diaspora. I wasn't alone.

Many of us had grown up with the poetry and teachings of June Jordan. We knew that those of us in the imperial core carry a responsibility to confront the twisted legacies of systemic hypocrisies by openly bearing witness and confronting the enemy when we face it, as Jordan exquisitely articulated in an open letter to her friend, poet Adrienne Rich. The letter, uncovered in archives in 2024, had not been published in the interim due to the tone policing of Jordan by friends and associates.[8] It is written in response to an open letter, titled ". . . What Does Zionism Mean?," of which Rich was one of seven cosignatories, all of whom self-identified as "Jewish lesbians/feminists of Eastern European (Ashkenazi) background."[9] That letter, published in response to public outcry over the Sabra and Shatila massacres of 1982, stated, "Zionism is one strategy against anti-Semitism and for Jewish survival. Anti-Zionism is Anti-Semitism."[10]

Jordan's response began:

> October 10, 1982
> First, let me be clear. Neither the word "holocaust" nor the word "genocide" was invented to describe the loss of Jewish or European life. Both of these words mean what they mean whether the victim is Jewish or not.
>
> Accordingly: Israel has created a holocaust in Lebanon entirely consistent with its genocidal aims as regards the Palestinian people. Indeed, the issue of the Palestinian people is the issue of the value of human life, per se, and, more specifically, the issue of the value of human life that is neither Jewish nor European. As the majority of the peoples of the world is neither Jewish nor European, it should amaze no one that we, Black and Third World people everywhere, attach fundamental importance to the question of Palestine.[11]

Jordan's letter, which ended with "I refuse to assume responsibility for your actions and your inertia. I do not accept you as my people,"[12] spurred a transformational moment for Rich, who, because of the admonition from her fellow poet, turned toward her responsibility and became an outspoken anti-Zionist and champion for Palestinian rights.

Another crucial piece of information had come in 2018, with the release of sections of a censored investigative documentary by *Al-Jazeera, The Lobby-USA.* Video footage leaked of the Israeli consul general, Judith Varnai Shorer, addressing the 2016 Israeli-American Council conference in Atlanta, Georgia, stating, "The major problem of Israel is with the young generation of the Black community."[13] This statement harked back to the "problems" Nixon faced with Black Americans, especially as the council was discussing ways to obstruct the Black Lives Matter movement, which, in 2016, had voiced its support for BDS activism that called for an end to Israel's illegal occupation of Palestinian lands.[14] In the leaked footage, Israeli diplomats went on to say that they were confident because there were senior Black civil rights leaders on their payroll who, they hoped, would help drive a wedge between older Black Americans and the younger Black Lives Matter generation.[15]

For me, the hardest bridge to cross was with the people not on the payroll who failed to make the connections, who questioned why we should care when we had problems of our own. All too often, it felt as if some of us were willing to do the CIA's or Mossad's work for them. June Jordan's statement in the 1991 documentary *A Place of Rage* was clear: "There are two issues of our time, really, that I think amount to a litmus test for morality, as far as I am concerned: one is, what you're prepared to do on behalf of the Palestinian people, and the other is, and what are you prepared to do on behalf of gay and lesbian people?"[16] Solidarity between movements, like locating the common denominators of the enemy, or pinpointing the articulation of the problem, is a threat to power. Yet, political education, or the lack of it, forges both necessary and unnecessary divides. Those indoctrinated out of class solidarity and seduced by individualist tropes, proximity to power, or "a seat at the table," are often the most popular voices. Thank the graces for Dr. Ruha Benjamin, who, in April 2024, at the convocation for her honorary degree from her alma mater, Spelman College, pierced the heavens in her keynote as she reminded, "Black faces in high places won't save you."

Chapter Eight

The Pledge to Resist and the End of Empire

Meanwhile, I noticed a video of my first public reading of "The Pledge to Resist" was beginning to circulate. I had contributed to its creation in 2003, in response to the US War on Terror, when a coalition of activists asked me to consider what a Pledge to Resist might sound like. I took the question seriously. I had refused, and taught my children to refuse, to recite the Pledge of Allegiance at school. So, the question I asked myself was what would I encourage my children or other youth in the US to recite? How could I, could we, address the responsibility of shifting the course of an imperial exceptionalist indoctrination? I had been weighing these questions long before and had just published "said the shotgun to the head," a book-length poem I had written over the previous four years addressing the exact topic. 9/11 had intensified the question, as propaganda swirled and it was clear that the US aimed to fulfill its resource-stealing mission using its power-brand of "freedom" to designate "savages" and "terrorists" at will. I felt that artists should dedicate themselves to writing new pledges and new anthems with the same commitment as those commissioned by the state to create military camouflage during World War I. This led to the release of the pledge on vinyl, with remix contributions from international DJs, producers, and visual artists, with the aim of providing a tool so that DJs could use their turntables as platforms to voice their dissent. The Pledge of Allegiance had the classrooms, but we had the clubs.

The Pledge to Resist

We believe that as people living in the United States it
is our responsibility to resist the injustices
done by our government in our names.

Not in Our Name
will you wage endless war. there can be no more
deaths.
No more transfusions of blood for oil.

Not in Our Name will you invade countries,
bomb civilians, kill more children, letting history take
its course over the graves of the nameless.

Not in Our Name
will you erode the very freedoms you have claimed to fight for.
Not by our hands
will we supply weapons and funding
for the annihilation of families on foreign soil.

Not by our mouths will we let fear silence us.

Not by our hearts
will we allow whole peoples or countries to be deemed evil.

Not by our will and not in our name.

We pledge resistance.

We pledge alliance with those who have come under attack
for voicing opposition to the war or for their religion or ethnicity.

We pledge to make common cause with the people of the world
to bring about justice, freedom, and peace.

Another world is possible and we pledge to make it real.

To make it real would require the crumbling of the US empire, an unlearning of all the stories it chooses to tell about itself, and, in turn, a rewiring and rerouting of the web of connection between the people on the land and the people *of* the land. Which is to say that as long as the settlers make the law of the land, the colony is not yet free.

> The almighty dollar, which when all is said or done is only guaranteed by slaves scattered all over the globe, in the oil wells of the Middle East, the mines of Peru or of the Congo, or the United Fruit or Firestone plantations, will then cease to dominate with all its forces these slaves which it has created and who continue, empty-headed and empty-bellied, to feed it from their substance.[1]

That these words were written by Frantz Fanon in 1961 should tell you all you need to know about *American progress.*

It is not enough to decry the actions of our government; at some point, we must take responsibility for those actions and put our bodies on the line to halt the massacre of Black and brown people whom the US and its allies see as expendable. Black death and Indigenous erasure lie at the core of the American project. Citizens across the Global North share this same sentiment, and, despite cultural indoctrination that still carries a veneer of racial superiority, hold a vision of a world beyond neocolonialism. We must connect our struggle with theirs—and, more important, with that of the global majority, if we are to crumble this empire from the inside.

I was asked to deliver a keynote address at the End of Empire and the Future of Freedom conference at the University of Santa Barbara, organized by the Green Party vice-presidential candidate and historian Dr. Butch Ware. The conference was the weekend before the 2024 US presidential election. Protests had succeeded in showing Biden's unpopularity, particularly with the Democratic Party's most crucial demographic, students. Kamala Harris was the first Democratic presidential candidate to be nominated without campaigning in the primaries since 1968, another year marked by unprecedented global protests, sparked by an assortment of social movements including civil rights, women's liberation, workers' rights, against compulsory draft and the US invasion of Vietnam, against state repression, and in response to the assassination of Dr. Martin Luther King Jr. The global protests of 2024 shared a singular cause: the multiple assassinations and the official charge of genocide against the Palestinian people by the State of "Israel," fully funded, armed, and supported by the US Democratic regime, the UK, and the EU. In the US, the student protests, which took the form of encampments spread out over 140 US campuses, were the largest recorded student "antiwar" protests in US history.[2]

Also similar to 1968, the Democratic Party did not nominate a candidate aligned with the students' anti-imperial demands. That year, after the June 1968 assassination of Democratic presidential nominee Robert F. Kennedy, who vocally opposed US participation in Vietnam, protesters outside the Democratic National Convention in Chicago were vocal in their opposition to the US imperial agenda and to the impending nomination of then vice-president Hubert Humphrey, who, like Kamala Harris, had made it clear that he did not oppose the military policies of the sitting president, Lyndon B. Johnson. The protesters were met with unprecedented violence by the Chicago Police Department, who used tear gas and dump-trucks as improvised tanks on protesters gathered outside the convention headquarters. The attack, later called "the Battle on Michigan Avenue," was captured live on air by television networks covering the convention. Demonstrators could be heard chanting, "The whole world is watching."[3] Poet Allen Ginsberg is among them, intoning, "Om," to calm the police. Poets at political rallies is a given.* Fifty-six

* Ginsberg's poem "Howl" had captured the voice and spirit of his generation and well beyond. That poem, along with Bob Kaufman's "All Those Ships That Never Sailed"—a poem Kaufman first recited in 1973, breaking his ten-year

years later, the whole world was again watching as the US-backed IOF conducted the world's first live-streamed genocide, with Palestinian journalists posting massacres as they happened, and cheerful IOF soldiers posting their own brutal exploits on social media channels.

▼

Following is the keynote address I gave at the End of Empire and Future of Freedom conference on November 2, 2024.

I feel like instead of "Not in My Name"*—which I wrote in 2003, in response to the US War on Terror—I should have written "Over My Dead Body":

---

vow of silence that had begun with John F. Kennedy's assassination in 1963—served as major inspirations for my poem "said the shotgun to the head." Kaufman coined the term "beatnik": as he recited poems while standing on top of police cars and being beaten by police (he was arrested at least thirty-nine times on disorderly charges), he shouted, "This is beat-nigger poetry!" Raymond Foye, "Introduction," in Bob Kaufman, *The Ancient Rain: Poems 1956–78* (New Directions, 1981); Kathryne V. Lindberg, *The Oxford Companion to African American Literature* (Oxford University Press, 1997).

* I had renamed "The Pledge of Resistance" as "Not in My Name" after I noticed the shirts worn by activists in Jewish Voice for Peace that read "Not in Our Name."

Over My Dead Body will you occupy countries, bomb civilians, kill more children, letting history take its course over the graves of the nameless.

Over My Dead Body will you erode the very freedoms you have claimed to fight for.

Over My Dead Body will we supply weapons and funding for the annihilation of families on foreign soil.

It is not simply an idea that one should be willing to die for their beliefs or principles but rather that there are hundreds of thousands, in fact millions, tens of millions, who have died at the behest of racialized capitalism and its imperial machine, which we feed with our labor. And if we are to bring the machine to an end, to halt its progress we must indeed be willing to face what Thomas Sankara faced in Burkina Faso, what Marielle Franco faced in Brazil, what Patrice Lumumba faced in the Congo, what Chairman Fred Hampton faced in Chicago, what Berta Cáceres faced in Honduras, what Steve Biko faced in South Africa, what Leonard Peltier has faced for forty-eight years in a US penitentiary, what Assata Shakur has faced for forty-five years in hiding,* and what Ibrahim Traoré of

* Leonard Peltier was released from prison in February 2025. Assata Shakur died in exile, in Cuba, on September 25,

Burkina Faso is facing right now. The fact is that the ruling class, of the imperial machine, is willing to kill and we must, at least, find the organizing strength to halt our labor and kill the machine.

Perhaps you do not know that the industrial era followed the colonial era and that all modern machines were built on the workings of the plantation, which is why, if you pull apart a machine to this day—a camera, a car, a vacuum cleaner—an engineer will describe the engine in terms of master and slave, even in computer programming. The word "robot," in its Slavic origins, means forced labor or slave.

It's a way of looking at why we were robbed of our religions, our culture, our God, our language, our familial relations. We tend to think, and for good reason, that they saw and treated us as animals, when one could also say we were the technology forging the new world—it was beaten out of us—in an attempt to make us robots.

We have worked under the command of a system, with no return not fought for, with petitioners and martyrs who said, "I may not make it to the mountaintop . . ." And here we are.

2025. "Leonard Peltier Released from 49 Years of Wrongful Incarceration," NDN Collective, February 18, 2025; "Black Liberation Activist Assata Shakur, 78, Dies in Cuba After Decades in Exile," *Democracy Now!*, September 26, 2025.

We have petitioned and cried to our government for well over a year now with no amends. What is left but to collectively halt our labor? Not to actually put our bodies on the line but to take our bodies off and out of the lines and means of production?

The media has coined a lot of terms over the past year. One of those terms is "anti-genocide protesters." But, aside from the rabid Zionists and the corporate heads of weapons manufacturers, etc., who profit from human extermination, who would not characterize themselves as "anti-genocide"? I imagine that even those who work in weapons manufacturing companies—not the owners, but the workers themselves—would characterize themselves as "anti-genocide." My point is, if they can fire weapons for almost four hundred consecutive days—and some of us allow ourselves to think, "It is out of my hands," "There's nothing I can do"—what would five days, five "business days," of taking what is in your hands, your labor, off the market, collectively, regardless of who you're voting for and regardless of who wins the election—could we bring the world and the brutal acts of our governing bodies, dictated by a corporatocracy, to a halt? What would it take for a just a moment of world-changing solidarity?

I know you can't afford to lose a week's pay, but we could certainly pool our resources and feed each other. I know you can't afford to lose your job, but if we could convince everyone on the job of the greater job at hand that we hold as humans—in particular, those of us within the imperial core—to challenge, to confront the role of empire, to stand in global solidarity, to halt the means of production, to take a collective vacation, to make a point, well, then it might reverberate loud enough when we say "Not in My Name." But, if it's just individuals finding the strength and clarity to stand up here and there—if it's just a few individuals who are "anti-genocide"—I mean, what is it the resistance says?

When they stand up to tanks and two-thousand-pound bombs and heavily fortified armies that spend munitions like singles at strip clubs—is the resistance's every act not a form of saying, "Over my dead body"?

This is not to put overemphasis on the role of death and martyrdom; it is to openly question what is the best response to an imperial machine that is willing to kill? That will record the sounds of babies crying and play them from armed drones so that anyone who feels empathy, who thinks they can help an ailing child, will be shot when they exit whatever "safe space" they have found? The ruling class weaponizes our weaknesses—I am simply pointing out theirs. They depend on our labor.

Now, some may say, well, Saul, you're a poet—what kind of labor can you withhold? That's fair. Usually, when I sit down to write I reflect on a phrase that Maya Angelou said when discussing a writing collective she was a part of in Harlem in the mid-seventies. What she said was that the point of critique for the writers in the group was "Anything an artist writes should be written with the urgency of what they would write if someone were holding a gun in their mouth." It's a wonderful point of interrogation for any poem. Could these be my last words?

Yet, the thing is, the ruling class behind the ruling parties is essentially holding a gun to our heads right now. I know that it not necessarily the case for everyone. For many, Palestine is way over there. Sudan, Congo, like Rwanda, is way over there. Haiti is way over there. Puerto Rico, Hawaii are way over there. I should not have to point out that the occupied land we now stand on is not some proverbial talking point, nor is it way over there. And when our relatives say Land Back, they are responding to the centuries-old and ongoing crisis. They are speaking directly to the climate crisis and what happens when those who hold no reverence for the land control the rights to exploit and destroy it. They are speaking directly to land theft and wage theft. They are speaking directly to the health and healthcare of the people, all people, and the environment. They are speaking to the racialized capitalism that has served as the foundation of the system we find ourselves under, to this day.

When the Lenni-Lenape were confronted by representatives of the Dutch West India Trade Company—the first multinational corporation—for the supposed "purchase" of Manahatta, now known as Manhattan, the idea of land ownership was not shared. In fact, it is said that Lenni-Lenape took the gift of currency as a way of saying thank you: thank you for sharing this land with us, for teaching us how to navigate the climate, for sharing your food, your hospitality; as a response to the many gifts the Lenape had given to the Dutch "settlers." But the Dutch were angry after they, in their minds, had paid a price for the land. They were angry that the Lenape did not take the sum and simply disappear. That they somehow saw the land and rivers as something that they would share. So, the settlers began to repeatedly attack the natives when they would come too close to their settlement and, in fact, decided to build a wall—a twelve-foot wall around their settlement—to keep the Lenni-Lenape out.

Now, within these walls—which they decided to charge other "traveling" Europeans, fur traders, etc., to enter—they established a market. At this market you could buy furs, horses; you could rent slaves—you realize that not everyone was in a position to buy one? Or two, or six? But, if you were building a house or tilling land, you could rent enslaved Africans for a week or weekend (some of y'all are flashing on those times you've driven through the parking lot of Home Depot, questioning "What are all these guys doing here?") Well, this market—where you could buy, trade, or barter goods; that the Dutch West India Trade Company built within the walls of their settlement on the island of Manahatta—still exists to this day. In the same exact spot and location—it is called the New York Stock Exchange—and you may not think you are buying or renting slaves when stocks rise and fall, but the global majority, whose coffee, whose rubber, whose sugar, whose chocolate, whose uranium, whose oil, whose fossils in precious mineral form, whose labor these stocks depend on, says different.

The wall that was built around the settlement no longer exists. The only thing left is the marker that tells you where the northernmost part of that wall was: Wall Street. The wall that was built to keep the Lenni-Lenape out. The root chakra of racialized capitalism and settler-colonialism exists to this day. Like the wall that is being built to keep out the Indigenous subjects of US imperialism, dispossession, and destabilization.

So, when I ask what would happen if we somehow found the collective solidarity beyond partisan politics, and the simple fact that many if not most would agree that genocide—particularly as government policy—is not "for the people," I ask it with the Lenni-Lenape and the many Indigenous peoples of this land in mind.

In his renowned essay on civil disobedience, the poet and essayist Henry David Thoreau stated, "Most of all I must see to it that I do not lend myself to the evils which I condemn." As a student at Morehouse College in the early nineties, much of my political awakening can be attributed to time spent on Spelman College's campus. It was there where 100 percent of the classes for my theater major were held, under the tutelage of the late, wizard-like theater director Glenda Dickerson. Our playwriting teacher was a woman named Pearl Cleage. Pearl Cleage had recently released her book of essays and performance pieces called *Mad at Miles: A Black Woman's Guide to Truth*, in which she provides a handbook for women in abusive relationships with men. At the tender age of nineteen, what first stood out to me was how she explained that she could not listen to the muted tones of Miles's trumpet without hearing the muted screams of the women he was notorious for beating and abusing. It was a lesson in a line being drawn between "a man and his music." I remember her list of signs that a man might become abusive, like "punching a wall during an argument," and her instructions to women on how to read body language and know when and how to get out of the room.

Perhaps the most memorable day in her class was just after the release of Dr. Dre's *The Chronic.* While walking across campus, Ms. Cleage had been shocked to hear a song blasting from a young woman's Jeep with the lyrics, "Bitches ain't shit but hoes and tricks, lick on these nuts and suck the dick . . ." Her lecture that day, clearly improvised and mostly directed to the young women in the class, was not only lambasting the abuse Dr. Dre had heaped upon beloved journalist Dee Barnes, but also of what it might mean to develop an abusive relationship with music. I and many of my classmates were transfixed by the conversation that day.

At that time, I was a dancer for a local rap group and spent countless hours on the dance floor in clubs, concerts, and parties. I'd enter a party and make my way to wherever the circle of hardcore dancers that drew onlookers had formed. I lived in those circles. Yet the conversation with Pearl Cleage had suddenly made me a critical listener of what I was dancing to, and I began not dancing to songs I judged as "blatantly misogynistic" as a form of protest, against the pull of my body. I found this to be nearly as difficult as dancing off-beat, primarily because some of those songs, like "Bitches Ain't Shit," had what appealed to me as the most intoxicating beats I had ever heard. Until then, I had no raging critique of popular culture, yet there, on the dance floor or rather a little off to the side, resisting bullshit in music, is where I began writing my first poems.

Critical listening does not necessarily reflect prudishness; it simply opens the gates of considering whether a particular song or moment is worth it.

You develop and nurture a radar and are perhaps less shocked—as abusers often tell you who they are—like when someone pointed out on X recently, discussing the "We should have known" factor in revelations about R. Kelly self-referencing as the "Pied Piper," or Diddy naming his label "Bad Boy," or, as Dee Barnes quickly pointed out, "Beats By Dre." The fact is abuse and toxicity are clearly evident for those willing to acknowledge it, long before court records become available to the public.

I connect that lesson to this moment—for one, because the feeling of seeing the mass of your people move one way while your conscience forbids you from moving the same direction can be isolating and marks one deeply. It has nothing to do with being contrarian or "a hater" and more to do with being tiresomely sober. The sudden embrace of "joy" and "Black joy" at the thought of having a Black woman as the head of the American empire—while that empire, her party, and her current administration acts to literally annihilate Palestinian people, while gaslighting about "ceasefire" after having blocked four proposed by the UN, meanwhile trumpeting a "Save Our Democracy" slogan from the very real and malicious incompetence of Trump and the coordinated greed of the right-wing think tank that marches behind him—is both valid and cynical due to the blight of genocide and the ways it has become ever so clear that it is not voters but donors, corporations, and the dated and racist strategic military interests of the US empire that rule the decision-making of the Democratic and Republican parties.

But y'all heard, "When people show you who they are . . ." and forgot that it's the ones who smile in your face, not simply the ones who never hide it.

Confronting abuse or "patriarchy" is certainly no less staggering than confronting empire. The blindness of the dance is the lack of acknowledgment of how it even came to be. The price of groceries did not become insufferable after October 7—only the price of the ticket. Ms. Harris did not win a primary, nor has she in any way distinguished herself from her predecessor. If she were standing at the podium because of Biden's actual incompetence, then she would have already been sworn in by now.

She is there, and some are dancing [regardless], because students, activists, and those who cannot or will not ignore the genocide of the Palestinian people have made it very clear that they will not vote for the perpetrator of the genocide. "Joy" cannot obscure the fact that, without an arms embargo on Israel and an assertion of the will to follow and not ignore international law, the majority of US voters are being held hostage by the Democratic Party, which is, in a very real sense, holding a gun to their head while slaughtering innocent people. This is clearly nothing to dance about—but, alas, where we find ourselves today has very much to do with another group of people dancing, for no good reason, outside of a concentration camp.

The most recent talking point has been that these were the leftists of Israel who purportedly dreamed of, I won't say "free," but perhaps better treatment of Palestinians—though it does not appear that any Palestinians from Gaza or the West Bank had been issued an invitation.

Yet, sometimes we crash parties with uncomfortable truths. When Dr. Ruha Benjamin was honored at Spelman College last semester, she had the courage to say (the now viral), "Black faces in high places will not save you." Yet, perhaps we miss the point when we highlight the "Black faces in high places" and don't interrogate the other half of the statement, "will not save you." From what? What is it that we might need to be saved from?

When the Last Poets released their searing critique of Black American popular culture, "Niggers Are Scared of Revolution,"* they said what they said. Dated as it is, the critique holds true in many of the

* The Last Poets spoke out with their art about racism, poverty, and other societal problems, starting in the late sixties, laying the foundation for rap and spoken-word poetry. "Niggers Are Scared of Revolution" was released in 1970 on the album *The Last Poets.* www.thelastpoets.com.

same ways that Dr. King confided his fears to Harry Belafonte of "integrating my people into a burning house." Far too often, the delusional desire for a seat at the table attributes Black faces in high places to the idea of progress, when the only thing progressing is the violence of empire, where we are now afforded the luxury of having blood on our hands, too, in a mission that would just as soon eradicate us if and when the bottom line calls for it.

If there is indeed some karmic retribution to be paid for the role of the white supremacist manifest destiny that animated the genocide and ethnic cleansing of the Indigenous of Turtle Island; if there is karmic retribution to be paid for the racialized capitalism that enslaved tens of millions of Africans and continues to underpay and imprison, with no retribution for "time served"; if there is karmic retribution to be paid for the rape of Puerto Rico, Hawaii, Haiti, the countless colonies, wars, theft that has instilled racial, gender, and class hierarchies; how do we distinguish ourselves from those who should and must pay? "'Will not save you' from what?" we should ask. Is it the fact that those mfs got what's coming to them? That it's out of my hands? It's above me?

I have no intention of telling you how to strategize your vote. I simply think that it is important that we acknowledge that it is not merely Trump and Project 2025 that should be interrogating an allegiance to a party that professes to be against right-wing book bans while refusing to tell the truth about Zionism and the brutal annihilation of Palestinians; that is overfunding and militarizing police, as police violence has only increased since 2020, and building dozens of Cop Cities across the country for US police forces to train with Israeli Occupation Forces; that is criminalizing homelessness while no longer pushing for Medicare For All; that is enacting "America First" abroad while lambasting it at home.

These are only some of the many inconsistencies of a political party that is dancing hand in hand with its power twin while holding the global majority as prisoners of its violent quest for resources and profit. And this is why many see it as extremely important that a third party, like the Greens, earn more than 5 percent in the upcoming election so that they can receive the federal and state funding that allows their candidates, and more importantly their policies, the attention deserved—for the technology of awareness that says that in order to achieve democracy, US politics should identify as "nonbinary."

However, although we cannot give Westerners the credit for inventing democracy, I do understand that, for some, voting for a party—no matter how distinct or radical—might be seen as a reformist act, an attempt at dismantling rather than burning down. Of course, and not simply because it is Native American

Heritage Month, we should consider what our Indigenous relatives might call a "cultural burning" or a "good burning"—a tool that was used to manage forests and replenish the land as a preventive to wildfires. The European colonial mind state saw this as a primitive act, neglected to understand it, and [we] are only now at the beginning of realizing the fortitude of ancient technologies in relationship to ecology which includes us, humanity.

But maybe it's too late.

Maybe we've ignored the teachings and voices of our relatives and our ancestors for too long. "Over My Dead Body" loses its force when, clearly, there are already too many dead bodies, under the rubble, under our prisons, under our skyscrapers, under our houses, and residential schools. These are the fossils that fuel a system that depends entirely on us, not just here in the imperial core but even more so in the countries whose resources the ruling class depends on. Maybe it should no longer be a question of our dead bodies, but the discipline we impose on our living ones, to withhold our labor.

If you have not understood that *power*, in its relationship to patriarchy, in family, in business, in education; in its relationship to capitalism, to living wages, to healthcare and basic services; in its relationship to white supremacy and its direct connection to visibility, suppression, news cycles, empathy, education, entertainment—that these forces have combined to enforce your silence on Palestine, Sudan, the Congo, and all connected atrocities occurring now and way before now, recognized and unrecognized, known and unknown, foreign and domestic . . .

If you do not realize that our talents combined, our voices combined, our monies combined, our dreams combined, our strengths combined, our love combined, our visions and imaginations combined, our labor combined, could generate way more change than your silence and fears combined, could generate a new world, an alternative energy that is not war, that is not material wealth, that is not comfort at the expense of—then maybe you're listening to the wrong music, watching the wrong movies, reading the wrong books, hanging with the wrong crowd, studying the wrong lessons, laughing at the wrong jokes, supporting the wrong causes . . .

And don't get it wrong, the future we are fighting for is the sovereignty of Indigenous peoples and lands here. It is to say that there is another future. That the science fiction that imagines aliens coming to colonize Earth is just a projection of the colonial imagination. Yet, there are higher frequencies just as there is dark oxygen in depths of ocean that sunlight has never reached.

When people say, "These are dark days," I hear "dark" as "powerful."

Over two hundred thousand dead bodies in Palestine. How many more women will take their own lives to avoid rape in Sudan? How many more bodies in the Congo and its deep web of mines? How many more missing Indigenous women? How many more trans lives? How many more prisoners as robots?

Zionism is artificial intelligence. Artificial because it does not teach life; it takes it. Nakba, take one. Nakba, take two.

But we were not supposed to see this. That's how I know it's our ancestors hacking the machines. The drum was the earliest form of wireless communication. It may not be true, but it sounds right. That's how music works.

Imagine. The most powerful five days this earth has ever known. What would it take to convince your neighbor, your schoolteacher, your client, your manager, to say, "We have the power to stop this." If we do it in the millions. If we organize—regardless of who wins, in solidarity with those here and abroad who lose either way.

We are facing an extinction-level event. The empire is exploding to prevent imploding. Yet, the inevitable rise and liberation of Indigenous people, of disenfranchised and marginalized people, remains at the core of the fears of empire. A lot of my friends and family who are sympathetic to the plight of Palestinians have consistently sent me reels and articles that boil down to "But Trump," "But Trump."

My response has been, These white people can choose whatever leader they want to helm their sinking ship. They respond, "But Trump," "But Trump," to which my question has always been, "Since when are we scared of white people?"

A few days after I gave that speech, Donald J. Trump became president-elect of the United States, after having been impeached twice in his first term and while facing thirty-four felony convictions in the State of New York. The same repressive course-correct that occurred after social movements led to the 1968 protests was now to be applied to a new generation, whose growing awareness of how US imperialism was rooted in its settler-colonial and racial-capitalist origins threatened the tightly choreographed dance of a duopoly intent on carrying on business as usual. The United States' home-brewed brand of fascism that inspired Nazism was once again to be focused on building and filling prisons, increasing surveillance, and empowering the lynch mobs to purchase ICE uniforms from Amazon, play cowboy, and round up herds of migrants to funnel into privatized concentration camps. There they would join the Black and Indigenous prisoners, disappeared by the state, erased from the collective memory, perpetually utilized by the corporate donors who benefit from their labor.

On July 4, 2020, in the "Salute to America" speech, during his first term as US president, Trump boasted:

> American heroes defeated the Nazis, dethroned the fascists, toppled the communists, saved American values, upheld American principles and chased down the terrorists to the very ends of the earth. . . . We are now in the process of defeating the radical left, the Marxists, the anarchists, the agitators, the looters and people who in many instances have absolutely no clue what they are doing. . . . We will never allow an angry mob to tear down our statues, erase our history, indoctrinate our children, or trample on our freedoms.[4]

The irony was that the young lawyer who sat whispering into the ear of Senator Joseph McCarthy in the forties and fifties, as hundreds of artists were blacklisted by the House Un-American Activities Committee (HUAC), later became the lawyer and mentor of the New York real estate developer who would one day become president. Roy Cohn was Senator McCarthy's chief counsel and had been a board member of the American Jewish League Against Communism since its founding, in 1948, when Cohn was twenty-one. The league was founded by ordained rabbi Benjamin Schultz, who led the attacks against Paul Robeson before the HUAC hearings in 1949.

Schultz's conviction was that "Zionism is incompatible with Communism."[5]

The generational memory wipe is a necessary function of the system.

Chapter Nine
Boosting the Call

I woke up this morning, and after about an hour of thoughts and reflections, I picked up my phone to see if there were any Palestinian accounts that had tagged me to share news or fundraising campaigns. The first image I saw was from Palestinian Pulitzer Prize–winning poet Mosab Abu Toha, sharing that the IOF was mocking two US artists who had voiced their concerns for those suffering in Gaza by writing the artists' names on two bombs that would no doubt be dropped by the IOF in the very near future. The bombs, which vaguely resembled elongated white bowling pins, read, respectively, "Go to Gaza, Billie Eilish," and "Go to Gaza, Mark Ruffalo." I scrolled down, and the next post was from Palestinian Emmy- and Peabody Award–winning journalist Bisan Owda, showing first-responder civil workers trying to pull people from the rubble outside the Nasser Medical Center, as journalists reported on a strike on the hospital that had just occurred minutes before. As they were reporting, live on air, another bomb struck, killing everyone we had just witnessed seconds before, reporting and working to save lives.

This epitomizes the climate, more than two years into a live-streamed, US duopoly–funded, –facilitated, and –condoned genocide. I cannot predict when or where this book finds you, dear reader. Yet, I know that the reckoning that the US faces, like that of the Zionist entity, runs much deeper than any regime change. Applying bandages to broken bones might make sense when it's a hairline fracture. We have witnessed the largest cohort of child amputees created before our very eyes. By now, if your sense of what this country is, does, and represents for literally millions around the world has not been blown to pieces, then you must be watching mainstream news, where, even when not state-sanctioned, the indoctrination and desire to salvage the supremacist notion of exceptionalism are so strong that it works in pure collaboration with the state without being forced. On the internet, the survivors and journalists held the bomb fragments right up to the camera. We read "Made in USA" with our own eyes. Within minutes, someone posted the factory where the bomb or bomb parts were made, and once again we were forced to reckon with the fact that people accept jobs as willing accomplices. They do not strike. They do not refuse to do the work. And when they do, the migrant class is swept in to take the place of the factory workers in the same exact way that

Black workers were swept in to break the strikes of white migrant workers in places like Chicago during the Industrial Revolution, in factories that until then had refused to hire them.[1]

This is the cycle of repetition, of events that should have been inscribed in your history books, along with visits to Indigenous memorial sites and a whole curriculum of imagined possibilities of planted trees instead of erected statues, the Indigenous songs you should have learned at school, African histories and folktales, the holidays celebrating slave and worker revolts, celebrating not independence from England but independence from the settler-colonial, Christian-Judeo, white-supremacist patriarchitecture of "Western civilization."

> The process of bringing people and lands that have not been civilized into civilization is the essential and vicious role of colonialism. When a State has consumed its available resources it is compelled to look elsewhere and to others. This is the etymology of colonialism; it is the language of domination, coercion, control, exploitation, assimilation, and annihilation. It expands and contracts in between breaths of unending wars, it colonizes memories to justify itself, this is what it calls History. Its corroded conscience constructs a national identity out of its insecurities: stories

> of greatness, of the world before and the world to come. It emerges entitled and assembles against its persistent enemies, the menace of those who refuse captivation, those fluctuating threats it names as "others."[2]

It is because this has not happened that we find ourselves in carefully crafted squabbles between two parties that differ in opinion on how best to carry out the imperial goals of their mission. With or without façade? Like distinctions made between those who do and do not take milk in their coffee, when the question is of coffee: Who grows it? Where? How does it get here? The easy comforts and rudimentary norms that inhabitants of the US and the Global North take for granted all come with sordid histories and realities. The rubber for your tires, the sugar in your coffee, the cobalt in your smartphone, the chocolate in your croissant, the diamond for your engagement, the gold for the ceremony, the Electoral College, and your Thanksgiving dinner all share genocide as a capital denominator. The wealth of nations, rooted in violent dispossession, has never strayed from its course. They have destabilized governments and killed thousands for banana splits. They do it now for cobalt, lithium, uranium, and oil. These missions are not hindered by internal elections. The manufactured consent is preprogrammed and perpetuated. The dead are hardly counted beyond their families and native histories. Meanwhile, new movies make waves and headlines. Their stars host *Saturday Night Live.* We're all in on the joke.

The ruling class is self-contained and self-reinforcing. What many of us inside the imperial core fail to realize is that regardless of wealth disparities within, to the global majority we are all "the ruling class." It is not merely a disposition of wealth but also of comfort, apathy, lethargy, and obliviousness—the trappings of privilege. The least privileged within the core, who know the language of dispossession, for whom life ain't been no crystal stair, did not appear as a series of choices, who felt the literal gun to the head, and hardly got by, barely got out, who are strangers in their own land, who share the privilege of understanding without interpretation, of not being shocked by the stories not in the news, not taught in schools—they've got their own stories. Untold stories versus ruling narratives. The untold are death sentences, a mass grave in each paragraph.

So, what is your role as an artist, reader? Your role as I see it is to process. Process the particulars of your observations and ruminations. Process the social and political indoctrinations of your upbringing. Weigh them against the state of humanity, or more simply, against your ability to become a better lover, a better listener, a better contributor to your society and the world that we share. This processing power can stir more necessary good into the world than any AI data center. The technology of human progress has been stirred by many artists who have worked to make sense of our emotions and well-being in relation to power, supremacy, and dominance. The often-unspoken role of art is to remind us that we are not alone in our feelings or observations, so if we are capable of making sense of jealousy, possessiveness, narcissism, insecurity, then we can surely outwit outsized ambitions to dominate and control—not only within ourselves but, once again, within the world we share.

Feed the process. Let your work fuel the struggle that has been multigenerational, multivoiced, and multinational. State-sanctioned capitalism and Black and Indigenous annihilation have too many cheerleaders. We need songs that crumble empires; films that teach, remind, and inspire; poems that would make a despot revoke your citizenship. It is a great thing to be honored as an artist; it is even greater for your work to honor those whose red carpets have always been blood-soaked, whose superheroes have always been labeled savage, angry, or "terrorist." The Western notion of superiority has served as the nemesis of human progress. Its "free market" has cost millions of lives. Do not use your precious voice to fight for a seat at that table. Do not imagine that the hardship your talent may immunize you against cannot be used to serve those who face nothing but hardship. Octavia Butler's novel *Parable of the Sower* seems to speak directly to our times. Notes for her unfinished novel, *Parable of the Trickster*, contain the epigram, "There's nothing new under the sun, but there are new suns." Here, the age-old wisdom of Solomon is brought into the new age. This is the role of the artist. Bring us forward. Help us transform ourselves, our will, our imagination, our power, and our processing power, into something that shifts the scope of possibility for our children and our children's children. Write new lullabies that immunize them against capitalist indoctrination. Understand that we are fighting age-old propaganda disguised as anthems, history lessons, and pledges, all there to do the silent work of convincing our descendants that there is nothing left to do but go along and accept manmade horrors as natural disasters.

For years, I've signed books with an epigram of my own. In it is my simple desire to see my work inspire in the same way that I have been inspired by the works of artists including Octavia Butler, Amiri Baraka, Paul Robeson, Nina Simone, Hafiz, Jimi Hendrix, Fela Kuti, and an infinite et cetera who have broadened the scope of possibility for me and countless others. I have been touched, healed, invigorated, amused, fueled, and charged by great works, which carried illuminated thoughts and ideas that shifted how I choose to live my life. That art can provide a touchpoint of inspiration and provoke the subtle transformations that bring new breath to old ideas, heightened insights into daily practices—these are the makings of the waves that will overtake the greed-fueled ambitions of the corporate and supremacist entities that view us as nothing more than pawns and consumers. It is not that I believe in the power of art; it is rather that I have come to understand the power of art. "May these words bring worlds."

Notes

Introduction

1. Humeyra Pamuk and Mike Stone, "US Has Sent Israel Thousands of 2000-Pound Bombs Since October 7th," Reuters, June 29, 2024.
2. Ahmad Absais, "Amazon Is Investing in AI-Assisted Apartheid in Palestine," *Jacobin*, August 21, 2023, https://jacobin.com/2023/08/amazon-ai-israel-palestine-apartheid-surveillance.
3. Assata Shakur, "What Is Left," The Freedom Archives, https://www.freedomarchives.org/Documents/Finder/DOC513_scans/Assata_Shakur/513.Assata.poem.What.is.Left.pdf.
4. Amiri Baraka, "On Art & Politics," speech, Binghamton University, April 20, 2004.
5. Josh Jones, "How the CIA Helped Shape the Creative Writing Scene in America," Open Culture, December 14, 2018.
6. Safiya Umoja Noble, *Algorithms of Oppression: How Search Engines Reinforce Racism* (NYU Press, 2018).

Chapter Three: Freedom Ain't Free

1. Gilbert King, "What Paul Robeson Said," *Smithsonian*, September 13, 2011.

2. King, "What Paul Robeson Said."
3. Jeff Sparrow, *No Way but This: In Search of Paul Robeson* (Scribe Publications, 2017).
4. Bill Kirwin, *Out of the Shadows: African American Baseball from the Cuban Giants to Jackie Robinson* (University of Nebraska Press, 2005).
5. Jackie Robinson, *I Never Had It Made* (Ecco Press, 1972).
6. Paul Emory Putz, "After Making Baseball History, Branch Rickey Faced a Spiritual Crisis," *Christianity Today*, October 18, 2024.
7. Johnny Smith, "Jackie Robinson Was Asked to Denounce Paul Robeson. Instead, He Went After Jim Crow," https://andscape.com/features/jackie-robinson-was-asked-to-denounce-paul-robeson-before-huac-instead-he-went-after-jim-crow/.
8. Smith, "Jackie Robinson Was Asked to Denounce Paul Robeson."
9. Richard Harrington, "Paul Robeson's Frontier Justice," *Washington Post*, February 18, 1998.
10. *Hearings Regarding Communist Infiltration of Minority Groups—Part 1, Hearings Before the Committee on Un-American Activities, House of Representatives, Eighty-First Congress, First Session*, 1949, pp. 479–83, Cold War and Internal Security [CWIS] Collection, J. Y. Joyner Library, East Carolina University.
11. *Hearings Regarding Communist Infiltration of Minority Groups*, 1949.
12. Martin Duberman, *Paul Robeson* (Ballantine Books, 1990).
13. Duberman, *Paul Robeson.*

Chapter Four: Violently Antifascist

1. Richard Schickel, *D. W. Griffith: An American Life* (Simon and Schuster, 1984).
2. "A 1905 Silent Movie Revolutionizes American Film—and

Radicalizes American Nationalists," *Southern Hollows*, podcast, January 28, 2018, http://www.southernhollows.com/episodes/birthofanation.

3. Desmond Ang, "The Birth of a Nation: Media and Racial Hate," *American Economic Review* 113, no. 6: 1424–60.
4. *Pittsburgh Gazette*, September 24, 1946.
5. Jordan Goodman, *Paul Robeson: A Watched Man* (Verso Books, 2013).
6. Goodman, *Paul Robeson: A Watched Man.*
7. Andrew Lanham, "When W. E. B. Du Bois was 'Un-American,'" *Boston Review*, January 13, 2017.
8. Paul Robeson, "Here's My Story," *Freedom* 1, no. 5 (May 1951), https://sites.dlib.nyu.edu/viewer/api/embed/tamwag_fdm000006.
9. Civil Rights Movement Archive, "December 17, 1951: 'We Charge Genocide' Petition Submitted to the United Nations," Zinn Education Project, https://www.zinnedproject.org/news/tdih/we_charge_genocide_petition/.
10. Giles Oakley, *The Devil's Music* (Da Capo Press, 1997).
11. "Things at Hand," *New York Times*, August 22, 1877.
12. Jeanne S. M. Willette, "Marxism, Art, and the Artist," Art History Unstuffed, June 11, 2010, https://arthistoryunstuffed.com/marxism-art-artist/.
13. Philip Foner, editor, *Paul Robeson Speaks* (Quartet Books, 1978).
14. W. E. B. Du Bois, "Criteria of Negro Art," *The Crisis* (1926).

Chapter Five: Race and Class Revelation to the Beat of the Drum

1. Stephen Brookes, "The Murder of Rio's Street Kids," *Insight*, August 5, 1991.

2. Boogie Down Productions, "My Philosophy," *By All Means Necessary* (Jive Records, 1988).
3. Boogie Down Productions, "Poetry," *By All Means Necessary* (Jive Records, 1988).
4. Winthrop D. Jordan, "Historical Origins of the One-Drop Racial Rule in the United States," *Journal of Critical Mixed Race Studies* 1, no. 1 (2014): 98–132; Matthew Wills, "The Free People of Color of Pre–Civil War New Orleans," JSTOR Daily, February 20, 2019; Cristal Nicole Eddins, *Rituals, Runaways, and the Haitian Revolution* (Cambridge University Press, 2022).
5. Thomas Skidmore, *Brazil: Five Centuries of Change* (Oxford University Press, 1999).
6. Cleuci de Oliveira, "Brazil's New Problem with Blackness," *Foreign Policy*, April 5, 2017.
7. John Trudell, *DNA: Descendant Now Ancestor*, album (ASITIS Productions, 2001).
8. At the time, my favorite pants were gray multistriped Girbauds, which I would fold over to taper tightly at the ankles, with a white, long-sleeve, button-down Esprit shirt and some Zodiac shoes with a metal toe cap—and don't forget the flip-ups. I also had to teach the local barbers how to give me a high-top fade.
9. Thomas Jefferson, "Notes on the State of Virginia," 1785.
10. David K. Shipler, "The Missing Paragraph from the Declaration of Independence," The Shipler Report, July 4, 2020.
11. Gregory J. W. Urwin, "When Freedom Wore a Red Coat," *Army History* no. 68 (2008).
12. "We Ain't Going," Kwame Ture, speech, Tougaloo, Mississippi, April 11, 1967.
13. Gerald Horne, *Paul Robeson: The Artist as Revolutionary* (Pluto Press, 2016).

Chapter Six: Zombification: Losing the Propaganda War

1. Junior M.A.F.I.A., "Get Money," featuring Notorious B.I.G. and Lil' Kim, *Conspiracy* (Big Beat Records, 1995).
2. Mehrsa Baradaran, *The Color of Money: Black Banks and the Racial Wealth Gap* (Harvard University Press, 2017).
3. Mehrsa Baradaran, "A Bad Check for Black America," *Boston Review*, November 9, 2017.
4. Baradaran, *The Color of Money*.
5. Baradaran, *The Color of Money*.
6. Daniel I. Weiner, "Citizens United, Explained," Brennan Center for Justice, updated January 29, 2025, www.brennan-center.org/our-work/research-reports/citizens-united-explained.
7. John Tierney, "Like 'Fahrenheit 9/11,' Except Bush Is the Hero," *New York Times*, September 30, 2004.
8. Weiner, "Citizens United, Explained."
9. Adam Liptak, "Justices, 5–4, Reject Corporate Spending Limit," *New York Times*, January 21, 2010.
10. Julian Brave NoiseCat, "The Western Idea of Private Property is Flawed. Indigenous Peoples Have It Right," *Guardian*, March 27, 2017.
11. Klee Benally, "Unknowable: Against an Indigenous Anarchist Theory," in *Black Seed: Not on Any Map* edited by Black Seed (Ardent Press, 2021).

Chapter Seven: Where Poetry Led Me to Protest

1. Lao Tzu, *Tao Te Ching*, translated by Stephen Mitchell, Columbia Teachers College Center for Teaching and Learning, https://ccnmtl.columbia.edu/services/dropoff/china_civ_temp/week03/pdfs/taoteching2.pdf.
2. Cedric J. Robinson, *Forgeries of Memory and Meaning: Blacks and the Regimes of Race in American Theater and Film Before*

World War II (University of North Carolina Press, 2007).

3. *Tantura*, directed by Alon Schwarz (2022).
4. Astead W. Herndon and Sheryl Gay Stolberg, "How Joe Biden Became the Democrats' Anti-Busing Crusader," *New York Times*, July 15, 2019.
5. Hassan Al-Assi, "Israel's Dirty Trade in Africa: Diamonds, Weapons, and Settlements," *Middle East Monitor*, August 2, 2017.
6. Al-Assi, "Israel's Dirty Trade in Africa."
7. "Diamonds in Israel," Observatory of Economic Complexity (OEC), https://oec.world/en/profile/bilateral- product/diamonds/reporter/isr.
8. Mariana Magloire, "Moving Towards Life," *LARB Quarterly*, August 7, 2024. The letter was found in the archives of Audre Lorde.
9. Magloire, "Moving Towards Life."
10. Evelyn T. Beck, Nancy K. Bereano, Gloria Z. Greenfield, Melanie Kaye, Irena Klepfisz, Bernice Mennis, and Adrienne Rich, ". . . What Does Zionism Mean?," off our backs 12, no. 7 (July 1982).
11. June Jordan, "June Jordan on Israel and Lebanon: A Response to Adrienne Rich," *The Massachusetts Review*, September 19, 2024.
12. Jordan, "June Jordan on Israel and Lebanon."
13. Max Blumenthal, "Censored Documentary Exposes Israel's Attack on Black Lives Matter," *Black Agenda Report*, September 12, 2018.
14. Blumenthal, "Censored Documentary Exposes Israel's Attack on Black Lives Matter."
15. Blumenthal, "Censored Documentary Exposes Israel's Attack on Black Lives Matter."
16. *A Place of Rage*, directed by Prabitha Parmar (1991).

Chapter Eight: The Pledge to Resist and the End of Empire

1. Frantz Fanon, *The Wretched of the Earth* (Grove Press, 1963).
2. Erica Chenoweth, Soha Hammam, Jeremy Pressman, "Protests in the United States on Palestine and Israel, 2023–2024," *Social Movement Studies*, October 18, 2024.
3. Joel Achenbach, "A Party That Had Lost Its Mind: In 1968 Democrats Held One of History's Most Disastrous Conventions," *Washington Post*, August 24, 2018.
4. Emma Bowman, "In Fourth of July Remarks Trump Attacks 'Radical Left,'" NPR, July 4, 2020.
5. Merle Miller, *The Judges and the Judged* (Doubleday, 1952).

Chapter Nine: Boosting the Call

1. Harry Haywood, *Black Bolshevik: Autobiography of an Afro-American Communist* (Liberator Press, 1978).
2. Klee Benally, "Unknowable: Against an Indigenous Anarchist Theory," in *Black Seed: Not on Any Map*, edited by Black Seed (Ardent Press, 2021).

About the Author

Photo by Geordie Wood

Saul Williams is an American filmmaker, musician, poet, writer, and actor. Author of *Said the Shotgun to the Head* and *The Dead Emcee Scrolls*, Williams is known for his blend of poetry and alternative hip-hop, and for his lead roles in the independent film *Slam* and the jukebox musical *Holler If Ya Hear Me.* Saul starred as preacher Jedidiah Moore in Ryan Coogler's *Sinners.* He was nominated for a 2026 Grammy Award.

Saul has toured in more than forty countries and lectured at hundreds of universities. He holds a BA in theater and philosophy from Morehouse College and an MFA in acting from New York University's Tisch School of the Arts. He lives in Los Angeles, California.